The Healing of the

Religious Life

The Healing of the

Religious Life

Robert Faricy SJ
and
Scholastica Blackborow

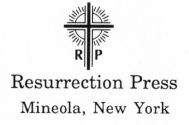

Resurrection Press
Mineola, New York

Published in 1991 by   Resurrection Press, Ltd.
                             P.O. Box 248
                             Williston Park, NY 11596

© 1986 Robert Faricy and Scholastica Blackborow

ISBN 1-878718-02-9
Library of Congress Catalog Number 91-60121

Cover Design: John Murello

Printed in the United States of America.

Contents

To the reader

We have written this book for men and women members of religious orders and congregations. It is meant neither for those religious who are completely satisfied with the way the religious life is going in their own lives and in their religious institutes, nor for the complacent; nor is it for those who, discouraged by changes in the religious life and perhaps by failures in their own lives, have lost all hope. This book is for those religious who, like us, know that the Lord is faithful to his promises, that the Lord does not want their religious institutes simply to go into oblivion, that we are in covenant with the Lord, and that he wants to guide us to new and better things for the religious life and for us religious.

This book, then, is for those religious who, even though they may walk among the ruins of what their institutes were, look forward to a rebirth, or refoundation, of those same institutes. It is for those who want to build, with the Lord, a new temple on those very ruins – for those religious who want to serve as stones in the temple's reconstruction. It is not for religious who consider themselves members of the last generations of their institute, but rather it is for those who want to think of themselves as already a part of what is coming, as part of the future of the religious life, and who see themselves not as the final stage of what has been, but as the first stage of what the Lord has already begun.

The pages that follow do not pretend to exhaust the topics treated. Rather, they indicate larger spaces. They act as fragments of a much broader vision that all of us can have now only vaguely, in a kind of cloud of unknowing, in faith. They suggest points that can lead to prayer, and prayer that can transform our lives. They propose a rereading of the religious life today and tomorrow, a rereading that stresses the lordship of Jesus and the power of his love. The pages that follow are pages of hope.

Scholastica Blackborow
Robert Faricy, SJ

No need to dwell on the past,
nor to think about the way things were
Look, I am doing a new thing,
Even now it's beginning
Don't you see it?   *Is 43: 18-19*

Foreword

One of my favorite stories from the Fathers of the desert is the advice that Abba Joseph gave to his spiritual disciple, Lot. The disciple came to his spiritual father and said: "Father, according to my strength, I sing a few psalms, I pray a little and my fasting is little, and my prayers and silent meditations are few and, as far as lies in my power, I cleanse my thoughts. Now what more can I do?"

The old man stood up and spread out his hands toward heaven and his fingers were like ten lamps of fire. And he said: "If you want, why not become totally fire?"

Most members of religious orders, brothers, nuns and priests are turning to their Lord and Master, Jesus Christ, their Divine Guide and Way to eternal life and are humbly asking what they must do to bring life into their dying religious orders and congregations.

A great deal of anxiety, discouragement and lack of hope is evidenced in the hearts of most modern religious as they face the future. The majority of them are over 60 with only a few young persons entering to replace the dying members. What is God saying about the future of religious life? Will the Church one day see religious orders and congregations as a phenomenon of the first two millennia of Christianity that gradually vanished as a dynamic force within the Church and the modern world?

Fr. Robert Faricy and Sr. Scholastica Blackborow tackle these questions in their small but valuable book *The Healing of the Religious Life*. As the reader is introduced to their realistic evaluations on the present state of religious life, she/he will be caught up in the deep paschal hope that is held out to religious communities and to individual members.

Karl Rahner has made an important statement that would describe the first suggestion of the co-authors to modern religious: "The Christian of the future will have to become a mystic, someone who has experienced something or someone, or he or she will be nothing at all." The authors stress the Vatican II decree on renewal in religious life *(Perfectae Caritatis)* that union with Jesus Christ is the essence of religious life. Religious who wish to revitalize their communities through the Holy Spirit must begin by deepening their personal, intimate union with Jesus Christ.

This is a call to modern religious to go beyond any heteronomous culture that might have locked individual members and entire religious institutes into legalism, uniformity and formal practices of piety and prayer which all too often prevented the development of a contemplative prayer life and greater surrender to the indwelling Trinity in the individual religious.

Using the dynamic of Pierre Teilhard de Chardin's analysis of structural process, Fr. Faricy deals with the life, death and resurrection to describe the movements of *integration* (where we have been), of *fragmentation* (where we are now) and of *re-integration* (where we hope to be going).

This work is full of hope and realistic optimism held out to modern religious and any Christian pondering the future of a dedicated life in a religious community. The message of this book can be phrased in the profound words of the poet, Francis Thompson, in his *Ode to the Setting Sun* which he wrote as he saw his own life slipping into a certain death with hope that death is necessary to enter into a new creative birth, leading to new life. He writes:

> *For there is nothing lives but something dies,*
> *And there is nothing dies but something live.*
> *Till skies be fugitives,*
> *Till Time, the hidden root of change, updries,*
> *Are Birth and Death inseparable on earth;*
> *For they are twain yet one, and Death is Birth.*

George A. Maloney, S.J.

Chapter 1

The Lord Calls Me

The heart of the religious life, and of all personal renewal in the religious life, is personal relationship with Jesus. That relationship consists in his call to me and my response. It is my religious vocation. I invite you to think through with me now, prayerfully, the meaning of your personal vocation.

What I am, and what I am becoming. Vatican II's Pastoral Constitution on the Church in the Modern World (Gaudium et spes) understands Jesus Christ risen as the future focal point of all history. We are headed toward Jesus risen, toward the point when all of us will be recapitulated, reconciled, under one Head. This is the meaning of history. In the contemporary evolutionary world view, the meaning of anything, what it really is, can be known only by what it finally becomes. I know what an acorn is because it will, or at least is designed to, grow into an oak tree. What is the meaning of history? That meaning is hidden in Jesus risen, history's future focal center. History has meaning only in him, and has no meaning apart from him. He is the Lord of history.

The same is true of me in my own personal history. I can understand myself truly only in the light of Jesus. My future is hidden in him. Jesus is my future and my meaning. I belong to him; I am his. The Father:

> *Has destined us in love to be his children through Jesus Christ.*

> *He chose us in him before the foundation of*
> *the world, and that we should be holy and*
> *blameless before him.*
>   Eph 1:5,4

I exist because I am (have been) called into
existence. That call which actuated the beginning of
my existence goes back before time to God's choice of
me. He chooses me. That is why I exist. What God
has chosen me to (finally) be in Christ remains to be
truly seen – in the world to come. My future is hidden
in him. Who I truly am is the person God has from
the beginning envisaged me to be. I am becoming who
I am. As the old slogan goes, "Have patience, God has
not finished with me yet."

My becoming – toward who I truly am – is the
result of God's calling me. It is my calling *from him –
to him* in Christ. It is my *vocatio*, my vocation. I exist
because I am called. My personal vocation is more
important than my existence.

What matters even more than my life is how I
respond to the call of the Lord, what I do *towards him*.
Today many persons consecrated to the Lord are dying
for him, martyrs, in communist countries, in Latin
America, in Africa – because their response to the
Lord is more important than their very life. I have met
a number of religious men and women in Italy and in
the United States who were on leave from Guatemala
and El Salvador and certain African countries where
the Church is persecuted. They were afraid to return,
afraid of being killed. But they went back, because love
is stronger than death. Faithfulness to my call from
the Lord, to my personal vocation, is more important
even than holding on to my life in this world. What is
my personal vocation? It is to be conceived and born, to
be baptized into Christ's body, to enter the religious
life, to live according to the charism of my institute, to
die in the Lord and to be with him forever. And that is
why I exist, the reason why the Lord made me.

Jesus needs me. God truly needs the world in this
sense: God and the world come together in Christ. A
fundamental mutual complementarity exists between

God and the world in and because of Jesus Christ. In Jesus, God is personally involved in the world– completely other in nature from the world, and yet unable to dispense with it. The world, then, can be understood as mysteriously completing and fulfilling the Absolute Being himself. This is what the Incarnation means. And this is fact: that God vitally needs the world, that the world somehow completes God. The fact of the Incarnation stands as the basis for the mutual complementarity between God and me in Jesus Christ. Jesus needs me. Because I am what he came for, lived and died and rose for. He needs me to complete himself. He needs me and each of us for his Body to be complete. He needs me; that is to say, he needs my response to him, to his call, to my vocation.

Jesus needs me, along with Paul, "to make up what is wanting in his sufferings." His need of me to carry my cross in union with him carrying his is traditional in Catholicism, and finds expression in the Stations of the Cross, in the concept of reparation to the Sacred Heart, and in many other ways. And he needs me to share with him in glory in the world to come, to be part of his glorified Body.

God did not choose to create the world and then later, as a kind of second thought, send Jesus to save it and later, as a third thought, put me into the world. He chose me in Christ before the beginning of the world. The world's vocation is to Jesus Christ. So is mine: I have been chosen in him, destined to be in him. It is all one package. The mutuality between God and the world, and the mutuality between Jesus Christ and me, are two sides of the same coin.

My involvement with Jesus and my involvement in the world go together. Jesus needs me to be complete, and he needs me to help bring the world to him.

The religious life: mystical or prophetic? My involvement with the Lord, centered on my prayer, my daily Mass, and my involvement with the world, founded in my community life and apostolate go together. They are really one. I can distinguish the *mystical* aspect of my life (my conscious union with the

Lord) and the *prophetic* aspect (my sharing him with
others). But I cannot separate them. The prophetic
dimension of the religious life makes no sense without
the mystical dimension. All forms of prophecy, even if
I take the word *prophecy* in its broadest sense, are
properly charisms, special gifts of the Holy Spirit given
to be used in building up the Body of Christ. This
includes the consecrated life as, structurally, a
strongly prophetic force in the Church. If that
prophetic force of the religious life seems weakened
today, in general or perhaps in my own life, the reason
is not hard to find. It is not to be found in a lack of
adaptation, or in a failure to go to the poor, or in lack of
courage or of talent or of discernment. Nor, for that
matter, because I am not following liberation theology.
Failure in the prophetic finds its cause always in
failure in the mystical. Jesus is the vine, and we are
branches. Without him we can do nothing.
What absolutely needs renewal in the religious life
today is its mystical dimension: contemplative
personal intimate loving union with Jesus Christ.
This is, of course, the Lord's work, accomplished
through grace and, in particular, through special and
transforming outpourings of his Holy Spirit. The
renewal of the prophetic dimension, also the work of
grace, will come consequently and simultaneously.
The prophetic depends on the mystical – without it,
prophecy is noisy gongs and clanging cymbals. With
it, prophecy becomes Jesus speaking and acting
through us in love.

Chapter 2

He Calls Us to be a People

He who opens the way will go up before them;
they will break through and pass the gate.
The king will pass on before them; the Lord
at their head.

Mi 2:13

God gathers us together as a *people*. He is the liberator who chooses the Exodus as his means of liberation, who asks us to be done with our own way of looking at things and calls us out of our own self-made security to walk with him in a hostile desert, fully confident in him who walks at our head – to walk together with our brothers and sisters; to walk together with the brothers and sisters belonging to other congregations, with all the faithful, without feeling superior to anybody.

Undoubtedly, a return to the awareness of our particular situation of election would bring with it the recovery of some of the values so deeply rooted in religious tradition. A text from Saint Peter's first letter (2:9-10) is particularly significant in this regard:

You are a chosen race, a royal priesthood, a
holy nation, God's own people, that you may
declare the wonderful deeds of him who
called you out of darkness into his marvelous
light. Once you were no people, but now you
are God's people.

God had freed some slaves in order to make a free people of them, a people which belonged to him as:

> *The first fruits of his harvest.*
> Jer 2:3

When promising his covenant, he emphasizes this:

> *If you will obey my voice and keep my covenant,*
> *you shall be my own possession among all peoples;*
> *for all the earth is mine, and you shall be to me a*
> *kingdom of priests and a holy nation.*
> Ex 19:5-6

Because of the covenant Israel will be Yahweh's personal and holy possession, a consecrated or holy people (the two expressions mean the same thing in Hebrew), a priestly people, because the sacred is intimately related with worship. The promise will be fulfilled in the spiritual Israel, the Church. The "non-people" will become God's people down through the ages.

Let us listen again to the words which ring out forcefully in our midst:

> *You are a chosen race, a royal priesthood, a*
> *holy nation.*
> 1 Pt 2:9

As God is the "Most Holy" and those who are consecrated to his service are called saints in biblical language, we religious can in a particular way identify ourselves with this holy nation.   And while this expression does of course refer to all the "holy people" who are called by means of baptism to a sanctity which is the work of God, by means of faith in Christ *(Acts 26:18)*, it is interesting to note that it is used particularly to designate the martyrs.   Now if we remember that the religious life was born at the end of the anti-Christian persecutions and as a kind of

substitute for martyrdom, we can see another reason
for considering ourselves his "holy nation."

There are many biblical texts which express the
mystery of reciprocal belonging between the Lord and
us, his people. In two particularly rich texts God
expresses an almost spousal affection:

> *You are a people holy to the Lord your God;*
> *the Lord your God has chosen you to be a*
> *people for his own possession, out of all the*
> *peoples that are on the face of the earth. It was*
> *not because you were more in number than*
> *any other people, that the Lord set his love*
> *upon you and chose you, for you were the*
> *fewest of all peoples; but it is because the Lord*
> *loves you, and is keeping the oath which he*
> *swore to your fathers.*
>
> Dt 7:6-8

> *Fear not, for I have redeemed you; I have*
> *called you by name, you are mine. When*
> *you pass through the waters, I will be with*
> *you; and through the rivers, they shall not*
> *overwhelm you...because you are precious in*
> *my eyes, and honored, and I love you.*
>
> Is 43:1-2, 4

The Lord, who is faithful to himself and to his
covenant, will never abandon his consecrated people
but, as in the past, he will bear them up in every
difficulty, make them strong, help them, and uphold
them with his victorious right hand (*Is 41:10*).

Does this mean the Lord will do everything?
Obviously not. In Esther's privileged position
Mordecai sees her precise responsibility and begs her
not to be silent but to take upon herself the destiny of
her people:

> *Think not that in the king's palace you will*
> *escape any more than all the other Jews. For*
> *if you keep silence at such a time as this,*
> *relief and deliverance will rise for the Jews*

*from another quarter, but you and your
Father's house will perish. And who knows
whether you have not come to the kingdom for
such a time as this?*

Es 4:13-14

Those of us who are consecrated also have
particular responsibilities to the great people to which
we belong. The Lord's intention is that we should be
the force of faith, the place where our brothers and
sisters can find and deepen their knowledge of God,
"experts in God," his witnesses:

> *'You are my witnesses,' says the Lord, 'and
> my servants whom I have chosen, that you
> may know and believe me and understand
> that I am He.'*

Is 43:10

We are required to be "in the world, but not of the
world": so deeply identified with our brethren as to
become one with their sufferings and their joys to the
point that we no longer struggle to find the right words
to intercede for them, and at the same time radically
different from them.

When we begin to realize that the institute to which
we belong is part of God's-people-on-the-move, we start
opening ourselves to a prophetic vocation which, in the
first place, requires our mentality and life to be
interwoven with the word of God. There is a prophetic
gestation period, it is true, on both the individual and
congregational levels. We need time. It is only
through suffering (in whatever form) that we manage
to transcend our humanity, which is so deeply rooted
in its own security and ways of thinking, and enter
into the dimensions of God, where we so often tend to
be exasperated by our incapacity to wait upon his time.
In order to be prophets, we need a prophet's faith.
Then the Lord will be able to enact the prodigies of the
exodus in the life of our institute, and our own life and
that of the institute will become an authentic

experience of the Living God, the Liberator who walks at the head of his people.

> *You are a chosen race...God's own people, that you may declare the wonderful deeds of him who called you out of darkness into his marvelous light.*
>
> 1 Pt 2:9

God did not choose his people by chance. He had a precise intention:

> *'As the waistcloth clings to the loins of a man, so I made the whole house of Israel and the whole house of Judah cling to me' says the Lord, 'that they might be for me a people, a name, a praise, and a glory.'*
>
> Jer 13:11

He is even more explicit when he speaks of:

> *the people whom I formed for myself that they might declare my praise.*
>
> Is 43:21

The Psalms, too, are rich in reference to his project:

> *Let this be recorded for a generation to come, so that a people yet unborn may praise the Lord.*
>
> Ps 102:18

A people who praise. It is David who teaches us, with a long string of verbs, what praise means:

> *Great is the Lord, and greatly to be **praised** and his greatness is unsearchable.*
> *One generation shall **laud** thy works to another, and shall **declare** thy mighty acts.*
> *On the glorious splendor of thy majesty, and on thy wondrous works, I will **meditate**.*

*Men shall **proclaim** the might of thy terrible
acts,
and I will **declare** thy greatness.
They shall **pour forth** the fame of thy
abundant goodness
and shall **sing aloud** of thy righteousness.*
                              Ps 145:3-7

But when do we in fact praise the Lord? When do
we declare the wonderful things he has done for us?
Which of our communities gathers together simply to
praise the Lord? Those who have tried to bring an
assembly of religious men and women to spontaneous
praise have learned how far praise is from our way of
relating to the Lord and from our way of being. Why is
it so difficult for us to break out in shouts of joy and
praise before the Lord? Perhaps because we do not
have enough experience of his power, because we do
not experience the exodus together, because we are no
longer guided by him, but by our own heads. In the
desert the Lord is his people's guide, day and night,
and this fact unifies them. And since they are aware
of the divine guidance, they are capable of praise. In
this connection it is worthwhile rereading the account
of what happened when Judah, under King
Jehoshaphat, had to wage war against a multitude of
enemies *(2Chr 20:13-30)*, of which the brief text that
follows forms the very heart.

*As they went out, Jehoshaphat stood and said,
'Hear me, Judah and inhabitants of
Jerusalem! Believe in the Lord your God,
and you will be established; believe his
prophets, and you will succeed.' And when
he had taken counsel with his people, he
appointed those who were to sing to the Lord
and praise him in holy array, as they went
before the army, and say, 'Give thanks to the
Lord, for his steadfast love endures for ever.'
And when they began to sing and praise, the
Lord set an ambush against the men of*

> *Ammon, Moab, and Mount Seir, who had*
> *come against Judah, so that they were routed.*
>
> 2Chr 20:20-22

It is praise that, recognizing the Lord as Lord, frees his power to act in our situation. So why do we not create, at community and congregational levels, times in which "one generation lauds his works to another"? Why do we not really try to open ourselves to trustful praise in every crisis, large or small? Praise acclaims the Lord for all that he is or does. It celebrates him. It looks straight at him and "claps its hands." Praise that glorifies the Lord is our reply to the glory he reveals to us, and it is because he created us for this that praise "straightens out" our individual and community relationships with him.

A people of faith. A community in which praise grows is also a community in which faith grows. The divine presence was rooted in the Exodus people, in their interiority or consciousness of being a people. They lived in the awareness that a father guides and corrects his children. And just as every people has its own constitution and codex of laws, they too accepted the laws and regulations God imposed on them:

> *Moses came and told the people all the words*
> *of the Lord and all the ordinances; and all*
> *the people answered with one voice, and said,*
> *'All the words which the Lord has spoken we*
> *will do.'*
>
> Ex 24:3

Recovery of the awareness of being a people-on-the-move-with-God implies the serene acceptance of norms and rules and respect for a person who holds authority, just as a foreigner who takes on citizenship swears an oath of fidelity to the civil constitution and to the head of state. If I really believe in God-who-walks-before-me indicating the way and speaking to me through a mediator as he did then, my reluctance to obey is incomprehensible. However, in order to reach this type of faith I must look for a new Moses, and my superiors must be ready to fill this role. As go-betweens, it is up to them to show to me, and to that part of God's people which forms my institute, the heart and thoughts of God which, like Moses, they have learned during his manifestations *(Ex 34:31-32)*. If, as mediators, they look to the Lord for words that motivate and build up, they will no longer reason on a solely human level. Psychology does not create a mentality of faith, even though it needs to be put at the disposal of faith if we want to help our brothers and sisters in their inner healing. God – and God alone – must be at the head of his people because *he alone is Lord*. Then there will no longer be "decisions to be taken," but a continual discernment of his will in everything, whether daily routine or something exceptional.

A people that has a sense of its own unity and interior life, knowing that its development depends on its members' talents, recognizes each gift as an enrichment for everyone and, far from wanting to thwart it, encourages its use in the service of others. When Joshua begs Moses to prevent Eldad and Medad's prophecies, Moses replies quite simply:

> *Are you jealous for my sake? Would that all*
> *the Lord's people were prophets, that the Lord*
> *would put his spirit upon them!*
> Nm 11:29

If only we were all prophets, capable of recognizing the prophets in our midst, overcoming every form of jealousy and bias, so that Saint Stephen's words could not be applied to us:

> *You always resist the Holy Spirit. As your*
> *fathers did, so do you. Which of the prophets*
> *did not your fathers persecute?*
> Acts 7:51-52

Paul's teachings ring out:

> *Do not quench the Spirit, do not despise*
> *prophesying, but test everything; hold fast to*
> *what is good.*
>
> 1Thes 5:19-21

> *Lead a life worthy of the calling to which you*
> *have been called.*
>
> Eph 4:1

> *Lead a life worthy of the Lord, fully pleasing*
> *to him, bearing fruit in every good work and*
> *increasing in the knowledge of God. May*
> *you be strengthened with all power,*
> *according to his glorious might, for all*
> *endurance and patience with joy, giving*
> *thanks to the Father, who has qualified us to*
> *share in the inheritance of the saints in light.*
>
> Col 1:10-12

The situation of the saints, as we have already
seen, implies divine promises. To the faithful people
heaven will reply with its favors; the Lord will come to
their aid in his merciful love and benevolence. If his
people listen to the divine norms and follow them,

> *he will love you, bless you, and multiply*
> *you;... the Lord will take away from you all*
> *sickness.*
>
> Dt 7:13,15

A people to be restored. "He will multiply you." But
where are the vocations? Have we perhaps saddened
the Holy Spirit with our unfaithfulness?

> *He went on backsliding in the way of his own*
> *heart.*
>
> Is 57:17

Let us return humbly to him, using the words
Hosea suggests *(14:3)* so that he will spread a corner of
his mantle over us once again, raise us up on eagle's
wings and fulfill his promises. Let us learn to offer

him – face to face – a new relationship of love and
faithfulness so that his steadfast love never departs
from us *(Is 54:10)*.

> *Thus says the Lord: As the wine is found in*
> *the cluster, and they say, 'Do not destroy it,*
> *for there is a blessing in it,' so I will do for*
> *my servants' sake, and not destroy them*
> *all...*
> *For behold, I create new heavens and a new*
> *earth; and the former things shall not be*
> *remembered or come to mind.*
> *But be glad and rejoice for ever in that which*
> *I create; for behold, I create Jerusalem a*
> *rejoicing, and her people a joy.*
> *I will rejoice in Jerusalem, and be glad in*
> *my people; no more shall be heard in it the*
> *sound of weeping and they cry of distress...*
> *Before they call I will answer, while they are*
> *yet speaking I will hear.*
>
> Is 65:8, 17-19, 24

We must not overlook the cluster of grapes image.
It speaks of union. If the Lord finds us united he will
be ready to listen to us.

Our institutes are, for the most part, in ruins, like
the walls of Jerusalem. As was the case then, our
enemies are plotting to prevent us from repairing the
breaches and are creating confusion *(Neh 4)*. As was
the case then, we must pray to our God and post
sentinels by night and by day. The walls will rise
again when prayer has taken its rightful place in our
lives again. In this regard, Nehemiah's decision to
entrust the job of a sentinel to half of his young men –
who would be most capable of reconstructing the walls
– is interesting.

> *And your ancient ruins shall be rebuilt; you*
> *shall raise up the foundations of many*
> *generations; you shall be called the repairer*

of the breach, the restorer of streets to dwell in.

Is 58:12

They shall build up the ancient ruins, they shall raise up the former devastations; they shall repair the ruined cities, the devastations of many generations.

Is 61:4

The walls will rise again and the Lord will be at our side. The entire book of the prophet Haggai celebrates the Lord as restorer. However, it sets out precise conditions for his intervention. In Isaiah we find the following passage:

Then you shall call, and the Lord will answer; you shall cry, and he will say 'Here I am'. If you take away from the midst of you the yoke, the pointing of the finger, and speaking wickedness, if you pour yourself out for the hungry and satisfy the desire of the afflicted, then shall your light rise in the darkness and your gloom be as the noonday.

Is 58:9-10

These conditions have great relevance for our communities today, particularly if we read them in a spiritual key, and we can add to them Haggai's admonishments:

It is a time for yourselves to dwell in your panelled houses, while this house lies in ruins?... My house lies in ruins, while you busy yourselves each with his own house.

Hg 1:4, 9

Is it not true that our usual interests and worries tend to be over material things or "family interests" rather than the reconstruction of the kingdom? Let us be careful to have the kingdom at heart, and the reconstruction of our institutes will be given to us as well.

> *These are the things that you shall do: speak*
> *the truth to one another, render in your gates*
> *judgements that are true and make for peace,*
> *do not devise evil in your hearts against one*
> *another, and love no false oath, for all these*
> *things I hate, says the Lord.*
>
> Zec 8:16-17

So if we proclaim our experience of the God of Moses and of Jesus, the God who frees, others will be attracted.   Many will come, in accordance with the Lord's promise:

> *Peoples shall yet come, even the inhabitants*
> *of many cities;   the inhabitants of one city*
> *shall go to another, saying, 'Let us go at once*
> *to entreat the favor of the Lord, and to seek the*
> *Lord of hosts;   I am going.'*
>
> Zec 8:20-21

When they recognize us as a people-on-the-move-with-God, people with whom one can experience his creative power, they will take us by the sleeve and say:

> *'Let us go with you, for we have heard that*
> *God is with you.'*
>
> Zec 8:23

Chapter 3

Faith in the Religious Life

God is with us. And I am called to faith in him, and also to faith in his active presence in religious community. While a religious is called to reach an uncommon depth of faith, worthy of a person living a life of special consecration, he or she must also firmly believe in his or her own consecrated life. This explains the ambiguous title of this chapter. In religious life faith is both confidence in the Lord and hope in the religious life. Further, one cannot separate faith, hope and love. Faith in Jesus implies trust in him. I place myself in his hands and this abandonment is an act of hope. Jesus is my hope already present because he is the promise of my future. Since to love means to give oneself to another, the surrender of myself to him is an act of love. Believing in Jesus I give myself to him in hope, which becomes love. Now the faith that hopes and while hoping loves Jesus assumes two essential forms in religious life: contemplation and community love.

Faith and contemplation. If contemplation is the first form in which my faith expresses itself, I can ask myself what it means to be called to contemplation. The risen Jesus calls me by name. I exist because the Father called me into existence in and for Jesus and to grow in union with him. So union with Jesus is the very meaning of my existence. From the beginning of time I have been called to be *this* religious destined to grow in union with Jesus in *this* particular institute.

This is my identity! The meaning of my real self is: myself-in-relationship-to-Jesus. As the Lord Jesus is the fullness of my existence and of its meaning, the central relationship in my life must be with him. My relationship with Jesus can and must give meaning and vitality to all the other relationships in my life and keep them going.

However, my relationship with him, like all interpersonal relationships, requires a presence if it is to be lasting. The Lord is always present to me. I must be consciously present to him. Conscious presence before the Lord is called prayer. Thus, my relationship with Jesus is at the center of my life, and prayer is at the center of my relationship with Jesus. I am already objectively in relationship to Jesus because I depend on him for my existence. Prayer means turning to him in awareness; it means turning my objective relationship into a subjectively conscious one. In prayer my true identity emerges because it is my person-in-relationship-to-Jesus that is at the very center of my being. And that relationship is more important than my own existence because my very existence depends on my relationship with the Lord. Who am I? I am this particular person-related-to-Jesus. Prayer makes me aware of this.

When all is said and done, prayer – contemplation – is awareness of being before the Lord; it is becoming aware of myself-in-relation-to-God; it is faith becoming hope and love. The possibility of entering into an intimate, loving relationship with God present for me in the risen Jesus is a mystery. It is a mystery of God's love for me. In his love he sends me his Spirit so that I can pray. If I am not contemplative I cannot really be a religious either, inasmuch as the heart of religious life is this personal relationship with Jesus which does not exist without contemplation. All the saints, from Saint Teresa of Avila and Saint John of the Cross to Saint Ignatius, Saint Dominic and Saint Francis have stated that the sense of religious life lies in this: Jesus is everything!

I am not saying that Jesus occupies the first place in my life. Jesus is in the first, second, third and tenth places because he is everything for me. Jesus is all or nothing. If I am a consecrated person I belong to him. I want only him, because he is enough for me. There is only one *all*. If I do not have this *all* I have nothing. I leave all the rest for him:

> *For his sake I have suffered the loss of all*
> *things, and count them as refuse, in order*
> *that I may gain Christ and be found in him.*
> Phil 3:8-9

He loves me and has chosen me for himself. This does not mean that I must not love the brothers and sisters in my community, and everyone, and all of creation. It is true that I must love everyone and everything, but with an open hand. I must love all and everyone freely, in Jesus, and in his way, with that interior freedom that the Lord gives me because I do not want to possess anything before him.

> *So through God you are no longer a slave but a*
> *son, and if a son then an heir.*
> Gal 4:7

He is my fortune. He is all that I have, and I do not want anything else. Not that I do not have other things. The point is that I have him, and this is enough.

Do I feel that I love someone too much? No. It is simply that I love them badly, selfishly, for my own gratification, treating them sometimes like things and not allowing them to be free. The real problem is not that of loving too much, but of loving badly. I need to learn to love a lot, greatly, but with an open hand and a free heart, without possessing or manipulating. The problem is my possessiveness, not love. Love is the solution: to love everyone and everything, in Jesus. Jesus is everything for me, and contemplation means living out my relationship with him in a concrete way which is both human and supernatural at the same time. This is why I cannot reach contemplation by wanting to and trying to but only by wanting and

looking for Jesus. It is a gift – his gift to me. I can
only put myself in the right frame of mind to accept it
and to grow in it.
Knowing Jesus through love. In my private,
contemplative prayer I make an act of faith by which I
know Jesus; by putting myself in his hands in hope I
know him by means of love. This is contemplation.
Springing from the loving knowledge of Jesus, it is
non-conceptualized, non-intellectual prayer. It is
prayer of the heart. It flows from the simplicity of the
heart, not from the head. Jesus wants my heart. He
wants my intelligence, too, it is true. But it is above all
my heart that he wants to possess. This is why he
wants me to be a contemplative.
Saint Ignatius of Loyola teaches me that at the
beginning of any contemplative prayer I should pray
like this:

> Lord Jesus, give me the grace to know you
> better so that I can love you more deeply and
> follow you more faithfully.

To love means to follow; but it also means to know
by means of love, giving myself to Jesus who gives
himself to me. I am in Jesus' presence. He and I. He
loves me and that is enough for me. I rest in his love
for me. The state of resting in him is a grace I can ask
for. When and as he wants, he will give himself to me
more deeply through graces of contemplation.
I can contemplate Jesus as the Gospels present
him. It is important to begin my prayer by
submerging myself in his presence so that I can come
into deep contact with him. Many religious who have
the gift of tongues begin by praying in tongues for a few
minutes. Prayer in tongues, like silent contemplation,
is non-conceptual prayer; it is looking with love on
Love. When I speak or sing in tongues I do not utter
sounds that represent concepts, but senseless
syllables, like the babbling of a small child learning to
talk. The sounds express the sentiments of love,
gratitude, praise and wonder that I am unable to put
into words. Prayer in tongues, being non-conceptual

prayer – looking at the Lord with love – is contemplation. It is vocalized contemplation. Singing in tongues is sung contemplation. Praying in tongues or silently I enter in awareness into Jesus' presence. Then I read the Gospel text, freely using my imagination to re-create the scene before my eyes, and I ask Jesus for the grace to know him better, love him more deeply and follow him more closely. And I remain with him in loving silence. The key to contemplation is not to be found in doing something.

I simply look at the Lord and let him act. I let him love me in the way he wants to in that moment: in silence, or in making me aware of his presence, or in showing me something of the wonders that are hidden in him. The key is not my remembering what Jesus said or did, but that he remembers. He remembers everything. Risen, he is with me in my prayer to share his memories of what the Gospel recounts. To express it with an image which is also a reality, I can let Jesus take me into his heart. In the intimacy of his heart he shares with me the memories of that particular event of his life as he sees it now.

I rest there while he draws me gently to himself and into the memory of what he did, of what he said, of what he underwent. I can repeat the name of Jesus very slowly in my heart while I contemplate the event, seeing it in a vague, obscure sort of way with the eyes of pure faith. Or I can surrender my imagination to him so that he can show and tell me what happened. We are not talking about corporeal senses, but about interior ones, above all the interior taste of the mystery. Whichever way he decides, I let him guide me peacefully. He is here with me, even if I am in the deepest darkness or the worst possible dryness.

> Lord Jesus, teach me to pray, to enter into a loving interpersonal relationship with you. Teach me of your immense love for me and of the fact that you call me personally, by name, to intimate union with you. Teach me to be aware of my total dependence on you and of your love for me. Help me to understand

that you are my fullness and my future, that
the meaning of my life is in you.
You have called me by name into existence.
You have called me to religious life and to
receive a new sending of your Spirit and his
gifts. May I enter into that deeper
relationship with you that you are calling me
to by name.

Amen.

Faith and community. My love for the community
is the second way in which my faith manifests itself.
If we are all to love one another, this applies all the
more to the members of the same religious
community. I am supposed to love each of the brothers
and sisters the Lord has given me in my local
community, one by one, just as he does. It is true that
this is not easy; and perhaps one of the things that
make it even more difficult is my lack of faith and hope
in the future of the institute. When I am discouraged
because of the scarcity of vocations, or what I see
around me in the community, or maybe even mistakes
made in good faith by my superiors, or when I am
discouraged and forget that discouragement does not
come from the Lord, then love in the community
becomes even more difficult.

It is the Lord who founded my institute; he himself
has always guided it and is still doing so now. He
leads it according to a law inherent in everything in
existence: birth, growth, life and then death. But after
death there is resurrection. And in the case of a
religious institute this comes about through re-
foundation. The important thing is that I should take
part in this re-foundation, that I should be one of the
living stones used by the Builder, even if it means
being cut and molded.

This hope in a new life for my institute is hope in
Jesus and in his power. With this hope I can look at
the future with confidence.

Chapter 4

Healing in Community

*That which we have seen and heard we
proclaim also to you, so that you may have
fellowship with us; and our fellowship is
with the Father and with his Son Jesus Christ.*

1Jn 1:3

Religious life as a life of communion. Each of our
communities should be able to share in John's boast
because, essentially, it is only the sharing of our
communion with the Father and the Son that gives us
any right at all to invite someone to join us in religious
life. We ask the Lord to send us workers for his
vineyard, but we often forget that his vineyard is just
this: *communion.* So are we the vineyard? Are we in
his vineyard? If not, God will never dream of sending
us vocations and the rebirth of our institute will not
come about. John continues:

*This is the message we have heard from him
and proclaim to you, that God is light and in
him is no darkness at all. If we say that we
have fellowship with him while we walk in
darkness, we lie and do not live according to
the truth; but if we walk in the light, as he is
in the light, we have fellowship with one
another.*

1Jn 1:5-7

We might have expected to hear him say that if we
walk in the light we are in fellowship, or communion,

with God, but on the contrary, John points out that walking in the light implies our being in communion *with one another.* So we can invite others to come and share our communion with the Father and with Jesus and we know we are in communion with them because we walk in the light. And we know we are walking in the light because we are in communion with one another.

God is a mystery; if he had not spoken to us about himself we would know nothing about him. We could look at the stars and conclude that someone must have created them but many people have observed them and drawn a completely different conclusion. The very fact that we know something about him and call him Father is, therefore, a first sign of his love for us – love that wants to make itself known and enter into relationship with us, revealing itself as it does in the person of Jesus. To know the Father we must fix our eyes on Jesus, the visible image of our invisible God. All of Jesus' words and gestures are words and gestures of the Father. I may find his love and compassion moving, but just the same I have caught only a glimpse of the love in God my Father's heart. Even though he loves us in an absolute way, Jesus' human heart is only a sign of the love that burns for us in God's heart. As I contemplate him and hear him speak, I being to realize that his whole mission can be expressed like this:

> *I have manifested thy name to the men whom*
> *thou gavest me out of the world... I made*
> *known to them thy name, and I will make it*
> *known, that the love with which thou has*
> *loved me may be in them.*
> Jn 17:6, 26

Jesus comes to tell us that God loves us. It is a very simple message, and yet we would never have dreamt of it. God loves us. *God loves me.* How much? Jesus says:

> *The Father and I will come to him and make*
> *our home with him.*
>
> Jn 14:23

What a wonderful revelation of God! The Father, the Creator, the infinite majesty of God comes to make his home in me! I can only exclaim, like Mary: "How can this come about?" If I ask Jesus this question I will get the same answer she did: "*The Holy Spirit* will come upon you, and the power of the Most High will overshadow you." The Lord will make his abode in my sinful heart by means of the Holy Spirit that he sent as his first gift to *those who believe* so that they might contemplate his presence on this earth.

Many religious have not yet grasped the fact that it is the Holy Spirit – and not we – who completes Jesus' mission on earth. And what is Christ's mission on earth? However we view it, it is the Spirit who carries it out, as we shall see.

Communion and sharing of spiritual riches. John invited us to participate in the communion of his Church with the Father and with Jesus. Communion is a concrete reality, a total sharing of life, a sharing of all the spiritual riches God has given us. Paul, for example, could not wait to share with the Romans what he had received from the Holy Spirit. In this way we build each other up in faith: your faith will be a blessing to me, and mine to you. However, are our communities places where we really do share our spiritual gifts and blessings? Where we really do participate in the communion of the Father and his Son Jesus?

God himself is community, three divine persons who share one life, one love. When he communicates himself to humanity, God creates among us what he is in himself; he creates a community, the Church. So the heart of the Church is this community of love. We must consider religious life in terms of community, too, by which we do not just mean a physical reality but the sharing of our communion with God, the sharing of the fruits of contemplation. We said that unless we are contemplative we cannot be true religious: we may now add that *unless we are contemplatives we will have nothing to share.* The lack of sharing in community is perhaps the consequence of the small amount of time we dedicate to contemplation. Yet the witness of communion and therefore of sharing is a specific form of witness that the Church asks of us today.

Community founded on the Spirit. Religious community is founded on the Spirit of Jesus; the love and union that circulate are a sharing in the life of the Trinity. Only God makes my community possible. It is not enough to be nice people trying to be nice to others. If the community is not in the Spirit it simply will not work. It is only our communion with the Father and with his Son Jesus that makes it possible for us to share their life and exult in it. This is the mystery of religious life. This is what we offer to others we may invite to come and join us.

Let us take a look at Jesus. The light of the Father shines out from what he does. Jesus tells us to do the same — to let our light shine out before others so that they see our good works and give glory to our heavenly Father. It is not a matter of inventing new works to be done. In his letter to the Ephesians, Paul tells us that we are God's masterpiece and that he has created us for the mission he has already prepared for us. So every good work I have done or have yet to do has been prepared in heaven since the beginning of time. In fact we say: "Thy will be done on earth as it is in heaven." God's will has foreseen the good works for us and now we carry them out on earth. And we do them in the same way that Jesus did: Through the power of the Spirit of God. We can only operate through this power. We can let the Spirit of Jesus complete his mission in us now. And as we do so we are being transformed according to his image, in a new revelation of the Father.

Love one another as I have loved you. This may seem magnificent, but words and ideas, however beautiful they are, are worth nothing if they are without substance, if they do not become reality. The Word of God was made flesh. When John tries to sum

up what he wants to say about God he simply says:
God is love! Love one another! There is nothing more
to say. God gives himself to us. The only way of living
our life is to love one another. The only life in the Spirit
is a life of reciprocal love. "Love one another as I have
loved you." There are no limits to his love.

Jesus has taken each one of us to himself as
individuals. He has *embraced* us. We have found a
place in the pierced heart of Jesus — each one of us,
with our own sins and limitations. And I must
expand my heart in order to take in every person the
Lord puts across my path, whoever it may be. I must
see him or her as my other self — as Jesus and the
Father see one another — and not as someone *different*
from me. My heart must be torn too, so that every man
and woman may find the way to enter and meet
Christ's love for him or her right there. I am unable to
love *like* Christ without his love, of which I have an
utter, existential need. *But his love — the love of God —
has been poured into our hearts with the Holy Spirit.*

When talking about what the Spirit would do for us,
Jesus said he would console and encourage us. How is
he going to do this? Most often through someone who
consoles or encourages us. This is the work of the
Spirit! Just as our soul needs our body to
communicate with, the Spirit needs us to lend him our
body so that he can complete Jesus' mission. When
did I last let the Spirit use me to console or encourage
someone? The elders of the Synagogue at Antioch in
Pisidia sent this message to Paul and Barnabas: "We
want you to talk to the people, if you have a word of
encouragement for them." Speak, if you have a word
of encouragement! What is my word like? Is it the
word of the Spirit? Every time I refuse to encourage or
console someone I go against what the Spirit of God
has come to do.

If there is a predominant sin in religious life, this
is it: we do not encourage one another in the Lord's
service. And there is no human being who does not
need encouragement, who does not need the Paraclete.
The Paraclete is the person who smiles at me, who
treats me as I should be treated. And I am the

Paraclete for others. If I refuse to be, I refuse spiritual
life. I refuse the action of the Spirit of Jesus in me.
Every word of encouragement or of consolation that I
say is a word of the Spirit. But the opposite is true, too.
Every word of discouragement is a word of the devil.
He, too, is a spirit and needs a body through which to
work. If the Spirit of God needs me to say a word of
encouragement, the devil, too, needs me to discourage.
The choice is mine, every day. And it is not an easy
one. Why am I so prone to negative attitudes, to
criticism and destruction? The psalmist answers:

> *You love evil more than good, and lying
> more than speaking the truth; you love all
> words that devour.*
> Ps 52:3-4

Love of devouring, or destructive, words exists. If I
ask myself why criticism comes so naturally to me, the
answer is that I love it. We always do what we love
doing.

Saint James tells us that until we control our
tongues we cannot live in the Spirit, because our
destructive words contradict the uncreated Word of
God. In his letter to the Romans, Paul takes a look at
the vices that constitute their world, their shameful
passions and carnal sins. Then he goes on to say that
God has permitted the corruption of their minds
because they refuse to conserve the true knowledge of
God. There follows a list of the consequences of a
corrupted mind: they are an easy prey to jealousy,
homicide, quarrelling, untruth and evil; they gossip
about one another. Paul is concerned about gossip.
Gossip is a fruit of the corrupted mind and the
negation of life in the Spirit.

> *Let no evil talk come out of your mouths, but
> only such as is good for edifying, as fits the
> occasion, that it may impart grace to those
> who hear. And do not grieve the Holy Spirit
> of God.*
> Eph 4:29-30

Paul makes the one depend on the other. The use of destructive words saddens the Holy Spirit, for the word, God says, is Christ our Lord, the creative Word of God, his redemptive Word. It is the only word we should use – the Word that creates, that builds up.

Chapter 5

Heal Me and I Shall be Healed

We are often tempted to think that it is the community that makes us what we are. Instead, we ourselves are called to make the community a place of healing for our brothers and sisters. So it is I who make the community what it is. And the community will be a place of healing only according to the measure of my own healing, in the depths of myself and in my capacity for relationship with God, with others and with myself.

Often the reason for the sadness that afflicts us or for the difficulty we have in relating to others is to be found in an unhealed memory: a hidden resentment, a repressed sense of guilt, and unconfessed sin that has been forgotten. The repressed memory of unaccepted suffering, or of failure, disappointment or frustration returns to the surface like an underground river in the most unexpected moments of our lives, disturbing our peace of mind and undermining our self-confidence. Praising the Lord in every moment of our lives, for all sufferings, failures, disappointments and sadnesses, as well as for every moment of joy and every success brings unhealed memories and hurts that have been hidden in our subconscious depths to the surface and makes us aware of them as hurts inasmuch as we are incapable of praising the Lord for them.

True enough, we suffer and we have suffered. We suffered as children and during adolescence. Maybe my mother did not love me enough, did not give me all the affection my sensitivity needed or did not give it to me in a convincing way. Maybe my father was too severe and demanding with me, too cold and detached, leaving an authoritarian father image printed on my imagination. Or maybe I was a sick child, with a fragile body and an overly sensitive spirit. Now there are the remains of that suffering within me, together with the hurts that were caused by it.

Psychology teaches us that the forgotten memories of our early childhood are the most important of our lives: conception, birth and what happened immediately afterwards. Birth was a very important event for me, even if I cannot remember anything about it. We often talk about the mother's pain, but the child suffers too. I, too, suffered when I came into the world, both before and after my birth. These memories have remained in my subconscious where I cannot get at them. But the Lord knows them and can heal them. How can I give them to him to be healed?

Jesus remembers, and he wants to heal me. It is not necessary for me to remember. He was present at my conception and he remembers. He was watching over me in my mother's womb and when I came into the world he was calling me by name. He was there then and he is here now because he is risen and transcends all space and time. He is present now, and in every moment of my life, to heal me of these memories. He wants to come into my memory, into these bad memories which hurt me and are at the root of the obstacles between him and me. In fact, most of the obstacles in my spiritual life do not depend on me: they are not my fault, but are hurts that have remained in me. They are hurts that his compassion can heal and wants to heal. There is no pride or timidity, resentment or rebellion that he cannot free me from; there are no problems concerning chastity, poverty or obedience that he cannot resolve at their roots; there is no bitterness or sadness that he does not know how to free me from, going back to their very beginning, to the memories that are buried and hidden, or even present to us.

Jesus wants to heal all these things infinitely more than I do so that my memory becomes what it was meant to be: the chronicle that preserves forever the history of my personal salvation and of all the infinite blessings I have received, to the praise of the merciful Father's goodness. What am I to do? I must put myself completely into Jesus' hands and penetrate with him into the solitude of my heart where I must let the power of his love that enfolds me love and heal me.

> *And I will betroth you to me for ever;*
> *I will betroth you to me in*
> *righteousness and in justice, in steadfast*
> *love, and in mercy.*
> *I will betroth you to me in faithfulness;*
> *and you shall know the Lord.*
>
> Hos 2:19-20

I let him regenerate me through this relationship of mutual, unmasked, loving knowledge which is deeply human and involves all the dimensions of my being: psyche, intellect and will.

> *I will be as the dew to Israel; he shall blossom*
> *as the lily, he shall strike root as the poplar.*
>
> Hos 14:5

Like parched earth, I drink the dew of his love, as I gaze on him. Whether or not I feel anything is of little importance. The Lord does not depend on my feelings, but acts in accordance with his own, which are sentiments of compassion and of merciful love. I confide totally in him, placing every sin or inordinate attachment or tendency to sin in his hands.

> *I will heal their faithlessness;*
> *I will love them freely, for my anger has*
> *turned from them.*
>
> Hos 14:4

With the help of my imagination I watch the Lord lean toward me and take me into the embrace of his forgiveness:

> Father, thank you for the wonderful gift of my memory, thank you because by its means I can recall all your many blessings. Forgive me for the way I have abused it, using it to harbor resentment, bitterness, hurts and unforgiveness. Lord Jesus, touch each of my negative memories and transform them into peaceful and grateful ones.
>
> Yes, Lord, you are merciful and you love me. Give me the grace to open myself to you, to put all my personal history into your hands. I give you my heart; I give you my body and my soul, my intelligence and my will, all that I am, that I have been and that I will be. Everything. Heal me! You can see my poverty and my need. I am sick; you are the healer. Come, Lord Jesus.

The outline of prayer that follows offers some suggestions that could call to mind the memories that have been repressed for many years in my subconscious. Jesus wants to heal me. I can collaborate with him by means of my imagination, dwelling on the memories that come to mind, seeing Jesus present with me in each one of them, and receiving his love, comfort, understanding and peace.

From conception to birth

> Come, Lord Jesus! Take me by the hand and walk with me through my life from the very moment of my conception. You were there, Lord, in that moment. If there was anything wrong genetically, or anything that could damage me psychologically, heal me now. You were there while I was being formed in

my mother's womb. You can see the things
that are still within me, buried in my
subconscious; the suffering which has
remained beneath the levels of conscious
memory: what I suffered for lack of space,
the difficulty I had in being nourished or in
assimilating nourishment, the smoking,
drugs, or drinking my mother did not have
the courage to give up, her precarious health
or psychological traumas, her tension or
worries, my having been conceived in an
unsuitable moment, maybe outside
matrimony. You can see where I need
healing. Pour out your love and your
compassion like water that gives life and
leads to flowering. Let it flow over me and
penetrate into me like a sponge. I do not
know what you are going to heal in me; I just
want to absorb every drop of your healing
love.

Childhood

I cannot remember anything about my birth,
Lord, but I know I suffered, that it was
difficult for me. All that light, the noise, the
strangers, the cold, hostile world. Heal these
buried memories. Let me hear your
reassuring voice calling me to life, calling
me by name. Take that little child I was in
your hands, hold me up to your cheek and
tightly to you so that I can hear the beating of
your heart. Comfort and console me, give me
the love that you desire so that I may be filled
with your love. And if my mother could not
feed me and had to have recourse to artificial
means, lay me on Mary's breast so that my
little hands can reach out for the contact, the
warmth and security I need and my eyes
encounter the smile on her face.

I can see you, Lord, at home where I used
to sleep and eat and play. Everything is

bathed in your presence. You are looking at
the child I was – moments of solitude, of
sadness, of misunderstanding and of fear.
Heal me, Lord, from all the hurts inflicted on
me during the first few years of my life.
Even if I have him no longer, I remember
my father as I saw him then. I thank and
praise you for his goodness, for everything he
did and underwent for me. But he was not
perfect. I want to forgive him now, in your
presence, for the times he humiliated me and
made me feel unwanted or inadequate, for
the times he caused me suffering because of
his absence, his misunderstanding and
severity, or by ill-treatment to my mother or
my brothers and sisters. In my imagination,
I move toward him and hug him, saying "I
forgive you!" Unite us, Lord, in your Spirit of
love and forgiveness. Heal our relationship.

Jesus, I can see myself with my mother,
and you are with us. Heal whatever may
have been difficult or wrong in our
relationship. She, too, had her own defects
and faults, some of which caused me a lot of
suffering: disinterest, impatience, anxiety,
complexes and things she would not talk
about, jealousy, preferences, hopes and
expectations I could not live up to. With you,
Jesus, I embrace her. Thank you for her
presence in my life. Thank you for having
chosen her for me. I thank her, too, and
forgive her, and if she is already with you in
Paradise I ask her to protect me and to pray
for my healing.

Help me, Lord, to remember in you all the
unhappy moments of my childhood. I offer
you everything you want to heal. When I was
little it was difficult and often painful for me
to socialize with other children and the first
occasions I was without my mother and the
family hurt me deeply. The others were often
hard and relentless with me or they

undermined my self-confidence, making
fun of me because of my weight, or height,
slowness or lack of intelligence and
vivacity. And school, Lord, was often a
torment for me, with the teacher who did not
understand me or who humiliated me, the
subjects I could not fathom, and the bad
marks, which, in spite of all I tried to do,
always disappointed my parents' ambitions.
But you, Lord, loved me just the same, with
my failures, my capriciousness and my
talking back, and now you want to heal those
hurts and remove all those things which are
rooted in my painful memories and
constitute an obstacle between you and me
and between myself and others. Heal me,
Lord Jesus, and I shall be healed!

Adolescence

I offer you the first ten years of my life, Lord,
so that you may heal them. Then puberty: it
was a very delicate time for me. Take me by
the hand now, Lord, as you did then, and
walk together with me through those difficult
years.

I understood almost nothing of the rapid
changes in my body and in my emotions. In
any case, little or nothing had been explained
to me because adults were inhibited then and
unable to see it all as an immense gift from
you. I was often ungainly or unpleasant,
stupid or impertinent without knowing why.
But you, Lord, understood me with all my
difficulties and humiliations, my ignorance
and even my sin; you understood me then as
you do now. You have mercy on the mess you
can see, and you forgive me. You forgive me
the things that I should not have read and the
bad friendships; you forgive what adults
may have done to me while I was an
adolescent. You feel for the solitude they left

me in, just as you do for the memory of
having been used by them which is still alive
in me. Heal me from my fears, from the
memory of the sins of my adolescence, from
the many times I was a failure, from all the
wounds inside me that go back to that time.

I am consecrated to you, Lord. If I have
any problem in the area of chastity, with roots
going back to those years of my life, heal me
in my chastity so that I may belong more to
you in a growing and joyful harmony of my
whole being.

Thank you, Lord, for my calling to follow
you in my religious institute. I offer you
these years together with the ones I lived
before entering religious life. I offer you all
the interior struggle that my vocation meant
for me, the suffering and division it caused
in my family. I offer you my unworthiness
of this gift. I do not know why you chose me;
perhaps because I had a great need of you and
of your healing. Glory to you, Lord!

The years of my formation

Thank you for the years of my formation,
during which I suffered a lot because I
understood very little and hardly anyone,
perhaps no one, understood me.

I can see you, Lord, in the house I lived in
during that period. Fill every room, every
place, with your presence. I entered for you
and it was you who called me. Heal the
memories full of solitude, humiliation and
anxiety. Relieve the pain which is still there
due to the doubts I had about my vocation, to
the scarcity of love I was shown and to the
difficulties I had in getting accustomed to
everything. Everything seemed so different
to me, so medieval.

Walk with me, Lord, through the years of
my formation and heal all the various levels

of my interiority. I am not asking you, Lord,
to be able to forget all these things. I do not
want to forget anything. I only want you to
take away from these negative memories all
the suffering and pain, all the humiliation,
all the shame and resentment, so that I can
praise you, Lord for the sufferings and
difficulties and mixed up things in my
formation. I have not always been faithful,
Lord. I have sinned and you know it.
Forgive me and heal me from the
consequences of my unfaithfulness. I have
been unfaithful in prayer, in my
interpersonal relationships, in carrying out
my duty, in chastity, in poverty and in
obedience.

But I have not left you, Lord, nor have you
abandoned me. Have mercy on me,
unfaithful by nature, lacking in love, weak
and needy. Heal the roots of my
unfaithfulness. Give me the gift of a new
freedom. Free me, Lord, from sin, above all
from not loving enough, from loving badly:
gratifying my own needs by using other
people, sometimes even in the name of love.
You know me, Lord, through and through,
and you understand me fully. I do not know
or understand myself. I do what I do not want
to do, say what I do not think, and am what I
never supposed I was. Heal me, Lord, and I
shall be healed!

It may well happen that in the days following this
prayer some memories return to the surface and
disturb my interior peace. This is a sign that Jesus
wants to heal them by taking away the pain, the
humiliation, the solitude, the anxiety, the sadness, the
resentment. I place everything in his hands so that he
can change the nature of these memories, freeing me
to praise him for all of them. As the memories come
into my mind I give them straight away to Jesus. I

can also look for someone to share my experience with
in prayer.

> *If two of you agree on earth about anything*
> *they ask, it will be done for them by my*
> *Father in heaven. For where two or three are*
> *gathered in my name, there am I in the midst*
> *of them.*
>
>   Mt 18:19-20

Healing of personal relationships. It may well be
that my relationship with some particular person is in
special need of healing. Though I was not aware of
this before, praying for the healing of memories may
make me so inasmuch as many of the surfacing
memories concern the same person. In this case three
steps in prayer may be useful to me. As they require a
good deal of cooperation from one's imagination, it is
best to assume a comfortable position in a solitary
place and pray with one's eyes closed.

1. Healing the root memory. Having been immersed
for some time in the Lord's love, I relive with all the
intensity I can the event which caused me the deepest
hurt. I take all the time I need to recreate the scene in
all its details. I see the other person and all they do,
hear their words and relive all the pain, sadness,
humiliation, resentment, unforgiveness, I felt then.
      I tell Jesus everything: I express all my feelings
and emotions with the same vehemence I would have
done then, without hiding anything, without any mask
of righteousness or stoicism. Then I go back a second
time to the scene, but this time I am no longer alone.
Jesus is beside me, watching me. I live through the
event again, noticing the expression on Jesus' face and
listening to his comments. Then I go back once more.
Jesus takes my place and relives for me what I went
through. I watch him carefully. How does he behave?
Exactly like me? And what are his reactions like? The
same as mine?

Lord, you behave very differently from me.
You are meek and humble of heart and really
believe that the Father loves you. That is why
you are not overwhelmed by the humiliation,
the offenses, the wrong, the violence, but live
through it, forgiving your offender. I can see
the meekness on your face as you gaze on
him (or her) with understanding. You know
why he acts like this and you have
compassion for him and love him. You do
not get bitter as I do. Give me your feelings,
your spirit of forgiveness. Let your
forgiveness flow through me to him so that I
can see him as you do. Give me your heart so
that I can experience your same love which
chose to die for him. Thank you Jesus!

2. Forgiveness. Forgiveness is a truly Christian
characteristic, but in spite of Jesus' example we have
great difficulty in forgiving from the depth of our
hearts. We often think we have forgiven while, in fact,
we still harbor traces of resentment or even
unforgiveness. We can ask Jesus to help us so that our
forgiveness becomes true forgiveness, according to his
heart.

With the help of my imagination I recreate the
place where I used to – or still do – find myself
together with the person to be forgiven. I observe all
the details until they are familiar to me: the
furnishings, the position of the furniture, doors and
windows, and so forth. I am in that room, but I am
not alone. There is someone else sitting in the corner.
They have their back to me. The atmosphere is tense
and heavy. I do not know what to say. What I would
like to say is too strong, too recriminating. I say
nothing. I feel ill at ease and begin looking around.
Suddenly I notice that someone outside is moving the
door-handle. As I watch, the door slowly opens and I
can see a person standing there. The figure is out of
focus to begin with, but it gradually takes shape until I
can recognize Jesus. He stays there in the doorway for
some time, hesitant. He is looking at us. Then, very

slowly, he enters and comes towards me. His face is
steeped in sweet sadness as he puts his arms around
my shoulders and whispers, looking me in the eyes:
"Why are you silent? Why are you not talking to one
another?" His eyes are questioning me now. I explain
everything to him. Jesus speaks to me: "Don't you
understand? Don't you realize why he (or she) has
done this to you? Aren't they hurt, too? And didn't you
know that I love him (or her) too – that I died for this
person?" He leaves my side and starts walking
towards the sitting figure. They are talking together.
I take in the expression of compassionate love that
illuminates Jesus' face. Now he is coming back
towards me, leading the other person by the hand. He
brings us together. "Forgive," he says to me. I stay
quite still, letting Jesus' forgiveness flood into me and
through me into the other person, and vice versa. I
drink in his love and his forgiveness, letting it flow
freely through me. Then, in Jesus' presence, I take
the other person's hand and squeeze it: "I forgive
you!"

> Yes, Jesus, I forgive with the forgiveness of
> your heart. Fill my heart with your
> forgiveness, because you always forgive
> completely. Do not let me harbor resentment
> or unforgiveness towards anyone again.

3. *Accepting the other person.* A sister witnesses:

> There is a third step of fundamental
> importance that the Lord taught me when my
> mother died. Our relationship had always
> been rather tense and painful; I had suffered
> a great deal due to her, both directly and
> indirectly, and even during those few days it
> seemed that all the pain had met on my
> doorstep.
> The day before her death I found myself
> praying like this: "Lord, I unconditionally
> accept all the suffering of my life that has
> been connected with my mother." It was

definitely the Spirit praying in me, because my own thoughts were very different. In that same moment all the weight that was oppressing me fell away and I found myself free to praise the Lord for all my suffering, for each memory. He had healed me! And not only that. I soon realized that there was no need to pray for my mother. I could go back to my usual prayer of contemplation because from now on she was *in* me, and whichever way I prayed she would pray *with* me and *in* me.

Accepting the suffering she had caused me, I had accepted her, too. As a result, I had freed her, and our relationship had been healed. I spent all the time that evening praising the Lord and contemplating what he was doing in me. What had happened to me?

Accepting the suffering, I had accepted its rooting itself deeply in me, almost to the point of enjoying it, not for itself, but because it was what Jesus wanted and permitted for me. Then, going round the "tree" that was taking root in me, I had discovered Jesus nailed to it, the same Jesus who healed us by his wounds — and I had been healed. Accepting the suffering, I had accepted once for all Jesus' love for me, that love that had chosen for me *that* mother, with all that the choice implied. And it is only love – the love of Jesus – that heals.

Chapter 6

Jesus' Word of Love Heals

Today we sometimes say that words have been devalued. Words have lost their meaning. They no longer communicate. This danger of devaluing the word exists in a more serious form for us religious.

Listening to the word. Daily we listen to the word of God, but often we hear it in a superficial way, as though we were unaware of the fact that the living God is speaking to us. We do not take it seriously. On the contrary, we often adapt God's word, reducing it to our dimensions. Without meaning to, in a subtle way we apply to it the consumer criteria which surround us – we exalt what exalts us, and we put aside what is uncomfortable. The word of the Lord is a necessity of his love: whoever loves, wants to communicate, to reveal himself, to the beloved. It is in the excess of his love for us that the Lord speaks, in order to speak to our hearts, to our spirits. And he asks us to listen to him because he *wants* to communicate with us.

By his Word, God speaks to his pilgrim people, to the part of his people that forms my institute, and to me personally. His intention is to create in us who listen, moment by moment, *a new relationship*, a more faithful and trusting relationship. Relationship is two-way. A word of love evokes a response. How can I respond to the Lord who lovingly speaks my name?

> *Take with you words and return to the Lord;*
> *say to him, 'Take away all iniquity; accept*

that which is good and we will render the
fruit of our lips'...
I will heal their faithlessness;
I will love them freely...
I will be as the dew of Israel.

Hos 14:2, 4, 5

So if I prepare what I have to say, and return to
him, he will be like dew for me, making me blossom
like the lily and spread out my shoots like a fragrant
tree of Lebanon *(Hos 14:5-6).*

If I want to live, I must return to him and renew
my mind in him, so that a new life will spring from
me to recreate the place I live in, my institute, society,
the whole world. The Lord wants to renew the world;
he wants to renew his people, his Church and the
various institutes that belong to it, but he needs us – he
needs you and me. It may seem a dream. What can
you do, weak and alone? You cannot do a thing. Yet it
is really you that he needs. If you begin to let yourself
be touched by the Lord, you will touch others and they
will do the same. The world is changed by contagion,
not by revolution. Unless by revolution we mean what
Francis, Dominic, Teresa, Ignatius, Rosmini and
Kolbe accomplished. To be touched by the love of God
and to spread it means letting ourselves be
transformed by God's Word.

Saint Paul says that the spirit of our minds must be
renewed *(Eph 4:23).* Having a new mind means
turning my way of seeing things upside-down. It
means starting to think like God, and giving up
thinking like the pagan world around me, or
according to criteria that have seeped into me despite
myself. It is he who renews my mind and shows me
how to live my life.

Do not be conformed to this world, but be
transformed by the renewal of your mind,
that you may prove what is the will of God,
what is good and acceptable and perfect.

Rom 12:2

The word transforms me. Mary knows that the word transforms. At Cana *(Jn 2:1-11)* she notices the situation at once. "Do whatever he tells you." Do everything he says. Carry it out *without discussion.* John's praises are precise: "Fill the jars with water." They "filled them up to the brim." They did exactly what Jesus said. "Now draw some out, and take it to the steward of the feast." And they did this. No discussion. The miracle of transformation takes place. If you do what he says, he will transform your life.

> *Receive with meekness the implanted word.*
> Jas 1:21

If I let my thoughts be similar to his, his word makes me *grow* as rain irrigates the earth making it fertile and causing seeds to germinate. The seed is the word of God; *(see Lk 8:12).* Look at the gardener: in order that the seed may grow, he must observe some indispensable conditions. Darkness, for example. When he wants to sow a rare seed, he does not throw it casually on the earth; he carefully prepares a deep hole, and then he hides the seed in the depth of the earth, in darkness. The darkness corresponds to my interior solitude. Within the earth there is heat, another condition which is necessary if the seed is to germinate. The gardener, who knows this, covers the earth with straw to keep the heat around his seed when the climate is particularly cold. The word, the seed in my life, needs the solitude of my heart in which to slowly take root, and it needs the warmth of welcoming love which comes in prayer. Growth requires nourishment. Just as a seed contains its own nourishment, the divine seed grows in me inasmuch as I nourish myself continually with the word – not human words; not books devoured, even if they comment on the word; not sermons or talks listened to with superficial enthusiasm; but *his* word mediated with love in solitude, in the darkness – which may mean aridity – of the depth of my heart.

*Mary kept all these things, pondering them
in her heart.*

Lk 2:19 and 51

The word must germinate in *my heart*. It cannot
germinate in my head. That is why the word of God
must be welcomed into my heart and not just into my
intellect. If one merely discusses God's word, without
faith in it as the living word of God, one judges it, but it
is unlikely that one observes it:

*If you judge the law, you are not a doer of the
law but a judge.*

Jas 4:11

The disciples of Emmaus *(Lk 24:13-27)* were talking
together, with sad faces. "We had hoped that he was
the one to redeem Israel... but it is now the third day
since this happened." This is an implicit judgment on
God's word. They are doubting his word; and God's
word, when doubted, gives sadness, not joy. In fact,
"their eyes were kept from recognizing him," and
Jesus admonishes them for being "slow of heart to
believe all that the prophets have spoken." Just as the
earth welcomes the seed, so must we welcome the
divine word as "the word of God and not as the word of
men" *(1Thes 2:13)*.

There is also an admonishment of Jesus which
Luke records and which we can easily overlook
because we are used to fixing our gaze on the
enigmatic words which come after it:

*Take heed then how you hear; for to him who
has will more be given, and from him who
has not, even what he thinks that he has will
be taken away.*

Lk 8:18

Jesus, who cared a great deal about how they
listened, called his disciples aside very frequently.
Perhaps the crowds would have distracted them. They
were to let themselves be transformed by the words, so

that their hearts could be free to listen to it and put it
into practice. The truth will set them free.

> *Thy word is truth.*   Jn 17:17

"Take heed how you hear." Yes, because you must
assimilate the word of God, not as you do when you
assimilate food that becomes a vital part of you, but like
the Eucharist: you must let yourself be *transformed.* I
shall know the transformation has come about when,
with Paul, I can say:

> *It is no longer I who live, but Christ who lives
> in me.*
>   Gal 2:20

I shall reach the full stature of Christ under
Mary's vigilance. Who more than she, the one who
was full of grace and chosen by the Spirit to give life to
the living divine Word, could comprehend this
mystery? She conceives the Word because she has
found grace, because her sheer beauty – sanctity –
attracted the glance of the loving God, and her trusting
heart freely welcomed the word of his messenger. The
Spirit wants to form the Word in me too. He needs me
to be Jesus today, but he will be able to use me only
when I have been transformed by the word of God.

Transformation through prayerful listening. The
Gospels show us a number of important meetings with
the Lord which teach us how to relate in a new and
deeper way with him through his word. Mary of
Bethany sits at Jesus' feet watching him without
missing a word of what he is saying *(Lk 10:38-42).*
Martha is busy getting things ready. Jesus tells her:
"You worry and fret about so many things, and yet few
are needed, indeed only one," which is tantamount to
saying: "Look for the Kingdom first." The Kingdom is
Jesus. He wants to be at the center of our lives. Mary
of Magadala, too, is at Jesus' feet; she covers them
with an expensive perfume and dries them with her
hair *(Jn 12:2-8).* She knows who Jesus is for her and
she has put him at the very center of her life. She no

longer counts the cost of what she does, nor bothers about what onlookers may think. Only Jesus matters.

Listening makes me grow in the knowledge of Jesus, in faith and trust in him, and in love. I let his word fill me and tell me what he wants to be in my life – who *he* wants to be for me and who he wants *me* to be for him.

This is what happens when Jesus meets the Samaritan woman *(Jn 4:7-42)*. While he is speaking to her about the "water of life" she is completely incapable of going beyond a banal, day-to-day interpretation of what he is saying. She does not understand. Jesus comes down to her level, and the conversation takes on a personal tone. Identities are revealed: having had five husbands the woman cannot say she is married. Obliged to look her own sin – shadowed reality in the face – by contrast she becomes aware of the Light. Jesus must be a prophet. A further contrast, between the old form of worship and the one that Jesus foresees, leads to the moment in which Jesus reveals his own identity to her. Seen in the light of Truth, mirrored in the Word, the sinful situation of the woman does not prevent her from believing. On the contrary, it becomes a starting point for her witnessing to others.

There is the rich young man *(Mk 10:17-22)*. As though it were an explanation, Mark puts this episode between the one of Jesus with the children and his words on the danger of riches, creating a contrast which helps us to understand the meaning – the difficulty that anyone rich has in entering the Kingdom is so very different from a child's simplicity. Children are so generous and like to share their things. They forget everything else in order to follow what attracts them. They are spontaneous and affectionate. The rich young man wants to do what is required of him. He is a religious–minded and devout person. Irreprehensible. The love of Jesus – which shines through his loving glance – asks much more of him. It asks him to take him seriously and to follow him. *The Word calls.* Just as the man in the parable sold everything in order to buy the field with its treasure, the young man must decide *where* his real treasure is. Is he willing to pay the price that Jesus asks of him in order to gain his closeness?

One thing is certain – the Lord wants more than my half-measures. He wants me to change something – perhaps everything – in my life. Zaccheus meets Jesus, and his life is radically transformed as a result *(Lk 19:1-10)*. He wants to see Jesus and in order to do so he is obliged to climb a sycamore tree. Their eyes meet. Jesus was looking for Zaccheus: he came to find and to save the lost. Zaccheus is looking for Jesus, but he chooses the wrong viewpoint. Jesus makes him come down and meet him on his own conditions. Luke lets us fill in the rest of the story with our imagination. Zaccheus sits and listens to Jesus, and pours out his own heart. When he gets up, he has decided to change his life completely.

The sycamore could be a symbol of the viewpoint from which I look at Jesus, at life, at others. If my listening-to-the-Word-in-prayer does not lead me to change radically, perhaps I am, like Zaccheus, in the wrong place. Am I trying to know the Lord? And if I am not succeeding, why not? What is my sycamore tree? Is it the tree of *activism*, which has its roots in ambition and pride? Or the tree of *worldliness*, which makes me judge everything through the world's eyes and according to its criteria? Or the tree of *selfishness*, which makes my search for the Lord be geared to some personal self-affirmation as a "good religious"? There is only one tree that lets me meet Jesus: the tree of *love* whose roots go deep into humility.

The Word heals. As I welcome and obey the word of God, Jesus makes his home within me.

> *If a man loves me, he will keep my word, and*
> *my Father will love him, and we will come to*
> *him and make our home with him.*
> Jn 14:23

The indwelling Word heals me. The psalmist sings:

*He sent forth his word, and healed them, and
delivered them from destruction.*
Ps 107:20

And the Book of Wisdom, narrating how the Lord
healed his people from the bites of poisonous snakes,
emphasizes:

*Neither herb nor poultice cured them, but it
was thy word, O Lord, which heals all men.*
Wis 16:12

Now the Lord's compassion turns to me:

*My child, be attentive to my words; incline
your ear to my sayings. Let them not escape
from your sight; keep them within your
heart.*
*For they are life to him who finds them, and
healing to all his flesh.*
Prv 4:20-22

When I look at all there is to heal in me and in my
institute, I must be neither resigned nor discouraged
about it. I must open wide the door of my life to the
transforming power of the Word-who-asks-for-my-love,
and let Jesus rule at the center of my renewed life.

Chapter 7

Renewal in the Religious Life

The Second Vatican Council's Decree on the
Appropriate Renewal of the Religious Life, *Perfectae
caritatis*, gives us three basic principles:

1. The religious life centers on Jesus Christ
   – he is the center. The purpose of the
   religious life is above all union with him
   (article 1). "Let religious, then, be
   faithful to their profession, leaving all
   things for Christ *(see Mk 10:28)*,
   following him *(see Mt 19:21)* as the one
   thing necessary *(see Lk 10:42)*, and let
   them concern themselves about his
   concerns *(see 1 Cor 7:32)" (article 5)*.

2. "The appropriate renewal of the religious
   life involves both a continuous return to
   the original sources of all Christian life
   and to the original inspiration of a
   particular religious institute and, also,
   adaptation of the community to the
   changed conditions of the times" *(article
   2)*. To return to "the original
   inspiration" of the institute means to
   recover, to renew, the charism of the
   institute as well as the charisms of the
   religious life as they are to be lived out in
   that institute. Along with this renewal of

charisms, the Council tells us, is a
continuous adaptation to the changed
conditions of the present age.

3. "We must take seriously the fact that
   even the best adaptations to the needs of
   our time will not bear fruit unless they
   are given life by a spiritual renewal"
   (article 2).

Let us take these one at a time: the centrality of
Jesus Christ, the changed conditions of the present
age, the renewal of the charisms of the religious life
and of the particular institute, the primacy of the
spiritual.

The centrality of Jesus Christ. To say the union
with Jesus Christ is central in the religious life means
situating the personal relationship between the
religious and Jesus as the heart and center of all other
relationships. This means that, if I am a religious,
then my personal relationship with Jesus Christ
should be the organizing principle of all the other
relationships in my life. Further, my personal
relationship with him should sustain and vitalize all
my other relationships. Religious renewal, then,
comes to this: it is a question of deepening and
strengthening the interpersonal relationship between
the religious and Jesus Christ. It is a question of
renewing not merely a person, the religious, but a
person-in-relationship-with-the-Lord. How can I be
renewed in my relationship with Jesus Christ? I can
be renewed in the processes of being in relationship
with Jesus Christ: of being united to him, of finding
him, listening to him, loving him and receiving his
love, and so on. I let him renew me in the processes of
living in union with him. What are these processes?
We can group them into three general sets of
processes, three sets of ways of finding and being
united with Jesus Christ in the religious life.

1. Processes of being united with Jesus Christ in prayer: personal, private prayer; liturgical prayer; informal prayer in common; recollection during the day; examination of conscience; and other ways of praying.

2. Processes of finding and of being united with Jesus Christ in community: in religious community; in the broader community of the Church; in the community of those we serve in the apostolate; in the overall communion of saints.

3. Processes of finding and of being united with Jesus Christ in understanding and evaluating the world, the reality, of which I am a part. I want to find Jesus Christ in all things. I want to see and be united with him in all of creation, and in everyone I meet, and in all my activities. And I want to evaluate everything, including all my possible decisions, in the light that he is. I want to know how to judge in the light of the Lord's love, choosing him in all my choices.

The changed conditions of the present age. The Second Vatican Council's Pastoral Constitution on the Church in the Modern World, *Gaudium et spes*, points out the "changed conditions of the times." Today the human race is passing through a new stage of its history, a stage in which proposed and rapid changes are spreading all over the world *(article 4)*. Further, the human race is passing from a comparatively static idea of the world to a more dynamic and evolutionary view *(article 5)*. The Church today tries to see the world in a contemporary perspective according to its duty to study the signs of the times and to interpret them in the light of the gospel *(article 4)*.

Entering into a more contemporary way of viewing reality, the Church sees too that, again according to *Gaudium et spes*, underneath all the changes there is something that does not change; the Church believes that these changes are anchored in the Creator and in Christ, and the the center and the destiny and the key to understanding ourselves and all of history is found in the Church's Lord and Teacher *(article 10)*. That is, Jesus risen stands as the future focal point of all history, of the world moving into the future. Jesus Christ is the goal of history's convergence.

This dynamic and Christological understanding of reality sees Jesus as center, as a center that pulls us always forward, that invites us to involvement in the future. This involvement in the future takes the form of service in the following of Christ, a service in the shape of the cross, cruciform. Moreover, the contemporary orientation toward the future implies a certain pragmatism; it underlines the idea of how-to-do-it instead of the idea of what-it-is. Contemporary persons are interested not in the essences of things, nor even in their existence. They are interested in what things might become, might be in the future, and in how to make them better. If the Middle Ages studied the present (metaphysics), and if the nineteenth century looked nostalgically at the past (romanticism), today we look to the future, pragmatically. *Gaudium et spes* points out how people of the present age get involved in technique and in technology in order to get involved in the future, in order to change the face of the earth towards a better future *(article 5)*.

Today, then, we find ourselves interested in "know-how," in process, in processes, in ways of doing things. This is true, too, of modern educational theory. In contemporary theory of curriculum construction, the emphasis is on the goal to be reached, and so on the teaching of the processes that lead to the attainment of that goal. And, according to contemporary ideas of constructing a curriculum to be taught, those processes (that lead to goal attainment) *are* the material to be taught, are the content. We can apply this to the religious life. The goal is intimate, loving union with Jesus Christ. The processes to reach that goal are: the processes of prayer, the processes of finding and being united to the Lord in community, and the processes of knowing and evaluating reality in the light of Jesus Christ. These processes are the content of religious renewal.

The renewal of the charisms of the religious life and of my particular institute. I meet Jesus, find union with Jesus, in terms of my own religious vocation to a particular community. Renewal, then, should help me to find Jesus precisely and explicitly within the framework of my vocation to the religious life as that life is lived in the order or congregation to which the Lord calls me. In order to understand clearly and adequately my religious vocation as a call to an intimate loving union with Jesus Christ and as a life of union with him, I have to understand my vocation and all that it contains in the light of his personal love for me. That is, I have to understand my personal vocation as his special gift to me. My consecration to him is not so much what *I* do (consecrate myself, give myself, respond to him) as what *he* does (*he* consecrates me, gives me the grace to give myself to him in response to his call). My religious vocation to special consecrated union with Jesus Christ is, above all, his special gift to me.

This gift of religious consecration is special, not given to everyone, but only to those whom the Lord chooses. It is a special way of being in union with him, of belonging to him. Further, a religious vocation is always a call to service, a gift for service according to the spirit and nature of my religious institute. This is the definition of a charism. A charism is a gift of grace, given to some but not to all, as a special way of being in union with the Lord and as a gift for service, for building up the Body of Christ which is the Church. My religious vocation is a charism. And the religious life is a charismatic way of life.

Traditionally in spiritual theology it has been customary to distinguish two aspects of the Church: the charismatic and the institutional. The whole

Church is charismatic, and the whole Church is an institution; the distinction between charismatic and institutional does not at all mean that these two aspects are separated or somehow belong to different parts of the Church. Nevertheless, spiritual theology has always found the institutional aspect of the Church especially concretized and manifested in the hierarchy of pope, bishops, and parish pastors. And spiritual theology has found the charismatic aspect of the Church especially concretized and manifested in the religious life. The religious life is charismatic. Each religious institute participates in its own particular way in the charismatic nature of the religious life. Each religious institute has its own charism, or rather its own special cluster of charisms that distinguish the way the religious life should be lived in that institute.

The Second Vatican Council, in its Decree on the Appropriate Renewal of the Religious Life, has emphasized the importance of the charism of the institute. The "fundamental norm" and the "supreme law" of every religious institute, of course, always remains the following of Christ as proposed by the gospel *(Perfectae caritatis, 2)*. This fundamental norm and supreme law is always a fundamental and supreme grace: to leave all things and, following Jesus in consecrated celibacy, to live with him in obedience to the Father even unto death. It is the basic charism of the religious life. This fundamental and supreme charism of the religious vocation, like a beam of light hitting a diamond and refracting through the diamond's different facets, takes a different form in each religious institute. Not, then, that each religious congregation or order has a completely different charism; each has a unique form of the one common fundamental and supreme charism of following Jesus in the religious life. The unique form that the basic charism takes we call the charism of the institute.

No formula can contain the charism of a religious institute. A charism can be appreciated, grasped, made somehow perceptible, only in people who have that charism. The charism of a congregation or an order is grace; and grace is personal relationship – in the Lord's power and love – with him. Charisms exist in persons, not really in words, in books or in documents. We can apply the general definition of a charism to the charism of an institute. A charism is a particular grace, given to some but not to all, for some useful purpose and as a special way of relating to the Lord. The charism of an institute, then, is the particular grace given (or at least offered) to the members of that institute, as an apostolic gift (including the apostolate of prayer) and as a special way to be in relationship with the Lord (in prayer and in other activities). The point is that the institute's unique charism is a grace given to persons.

The vows, too, are charisms. It is true that the religious vows of poverty, chastity and obedience are mentioned in canon law; they are juridical concepts. But not primarily: primarily they are charisms, special gifts. Sometimes writers and speakers discourse about the psychology of the vows, about the vows as human response to the Lord. They are his gift to me. Jesus *empowers* me to be united with him by being poor, chaste and obedient.

Poverty is a special way of being united with Jesus, poor with Jesus poor, and also a gift of freedom to serve him in others. It is the charism of leaving everything for Jesus in order to be united with him.

> *Jesus said to him, 'If you would be perfect, go, sell what you possess and give to the poor, and you will have treasure in heaven: and come, follow me.'*
>
> Mt 19:21

In the book of the prophet Ezekiel, the Lord says:

> *They shall have no inheritance; I am their inheritance. And you shall give them no possession in Israel; I am their possession.*
>
> Ez 44:28

Chastity is a charism, a special way of belonging to Jesus Christ as well as a gift of a certain kind of freedom for service, a freedom to love more, not less *(cf Mt 19:12)*. Saint Paul writes to the Corinthians:

> *I wish that all were as I myself am (i.e.*
> *celibate), but each has his own special gift*
> *from God* (in Greek, *charisma*).
>
> 1Cor 7:7

The charism of obedience unites me to Jesus in such a way that he specially empowers me to obey him speaking to me through my prayer, through the events of my life, through the Church, and especially through my superiors. It is a special way of loving the Lord and of freedom to serve him in others. My religious obedience participates charismatically in Jesus' obedience to the Father. In John's Gospel, Jesus states:

> *I can do nothing on my own authority; as I*
> *hear, I judge; and my judgement is just,*
> *because I seek not my own will but the will of*
> *him who sent me.*
>
> Jn 5:30

Jesus:

> *emptied myself... and became obedient unto*
> *death, even death on a cross.*
>
> Phil 2:8

There are other charisms, of course, in the religious life: charisms of living in community, charisms of apostolate (teaching, caring for the sick, administering, preaching, counselling, and many others), charisms of prayer proper to a particular institute. There are charisms of spiritual leadership, of governing, and of forming others in the religious life. All these charisms are ways of being in union with Jesus and of serving him in others. They are gifts to us that unite us to him and empower us to serve him in love. The doctrine of charisms is not new in the Church. Saint Paul writes about charisms and gives several lists of charisms. In his first letter to the Corinthians we read:

> *Now there are a variety of gifts, but the same Spirit; and there are different kinds of service, but the same Lord... To each is given a manifestation of the Spirit for the common good. To one is given through the Spirit the speaking of wisdom, and to another the speaking out of knowledge according to the same Spirit, to another faith by the same Spirit, to another gifts of healing by the one Spirit, to another the working of miracles, to another prophecy, to another the ability to distinguish between spirits,...*
> 1Cor 12:4-10; see 12:28-31

The letter to the Ephesians speaks of the charisms of prophecy, of evangelization, of pastoring, and of teaching *(Eph 4:11)*. To the Romans, Paul lists the charisms of ministering, of teaching, of exhorting, of presiding, of doing works of mercy *(Rom 12:7-8)*.

The Church has always had charisms, especially in the religious life. The Franciscan movement, beginning with Francis of Assisi, marked a great outpouring of charisms, especially those of poverty, of evangelization and of simplicity. Later, the foundation of the Jesuits witnessed to an outpouring of charisms, particularly of the gifts of obedience and loyalty to the Church. In the last century, the Lord poured out charisms of teaching and of serving the poor in several foundations of religious congregations.

The Second Vatican Council speaks of charisms in several places, and especially in the Dogmatic Constitution on the Church, *Lumen gentium*:

> These charisms whether outstanding or simpler and more widely diffused, since they are particularly apt and useful to the needs of the Church, should be accepted with thanksgiving and gladness. *(article 12)*

If charisms are so important to the Church, and especially to the religious life, where and how do they fit into the doctrinal content of formation in the religious life?

There is, it seems to me, a danger of understanding the history of the institute, the spirit and charism of the institute, the vows, religious consecration, as though all this were ideological material, elements of an ideology. The ideology of the religious life: Jesuit ideology, Franciscan ideology, Rosminian ideology. No. We do not have an ideology. We have Jesus Christ, not an ideology but a person. We approach and are united to him in different ways, according to our different spiritualities. But a spirituality is not an ideology. An ideology is abstract. A spirituality is relational. An ideology helps to understand and judge reality, gives principles of action and a program to be trusted in. A spirituality unites me with Jesus Christ; I trust in him; he is my program. Political parties have ideologies. We have Jesus Christ. He is the center and the foundation of the religious life in all its diverse manifestations.

The primacy of the spiritual. No one, of course, would seriously contest the primacy of spiritual renewal over every kind of renewal of the religious life. By the word "spiritual" I mean to designate those values, the "spiritual values," that refer directly to the spiritual life – to growth in intimate and loving union with Jesus Christ encountered in prayer, in community, and in one's everyday perceptions and evaluations. None of us contests the primacy of the spiritual.

Why, then, do I want to emphasize something that we all agree with? Because of the strong temptation today in many orders and congregations to substitute some sort of ideology for the needed emphasis on those processes that lead to closer personal union with Jesus Christ. We can, today, be tempted to teach ideological elements, such as, for example, the theology of liberation, or some socio-political theory, or perhaps a set of socio-psychological ideas. Or we can be tempted to teach the spirit and the charisms of the religious life as lived in our own institute as *though* they were made up of ideological elements. The temptation is to teach doctrine as ideology, as simply conceptual material in the abstract rather than food for prayerful and loving union with the Lord.

Why should such a temptation be prevalent today? Because so many orders and congregations today are in a breakdown period and seem to be coming to an end. In many orders and congregations, there are very few vocations; people even question the meaning and the validity of the religious life; there seem to be more personal problems than some years ago. The average age of the institute or of the province goes up almost a year every year. After a while, since young people can no longer identify with such an elderly group, the trickle of vocations dies out, and the province or the congregation dies out. The prospect that this might happen – or seems to be happening – can cause anxiety and provide confusion.

In particular, major superiors and those in charge of formation and also of ongoing formation want to do everything they can to revitalize the institute, to renew its charisms and its spirit and its life. They often establish committees to study the charism of the founder and the spirit of the institute. They sometimes send mimeographed study and discussion material to all the houses. In general, they try to relight the fires that animated the first generations of the institute. They try to recover the institute's original charism and spirit by a return to the origins of the order or congregation. They often try to do this by ideology, by discussion and study and documentation. It does not work. It cannot work. It cannot work because ideology cannot renew us. Only Jesus Christ can renew the religious life. Renewal means growth in intimate, loving union with him. Not knowing more, but knowing him better and receiving his love better and loving him more.

Chapter 8

The Death and Resurrection of the Religious Life

How can I understand what is happening to the religious life today? How can I have a better understanding of just what is going on in my own order or congregation, or in my province? I am a part of my congregation, and it seems to be in many ways in crisis. It may even seem to be dying for lack of vocations, for lack of leadership, from excessive work-orientation and over-institutionalization. Real understanding of the present crisis in the religious life calls for a faith perspective. Real understanding, given the religious nature of the crisis, calls for understanding in faith. I need to understand the story of the religious life, the story of my own religious institute, and my own story as a part of all that, in terms of the story of Jesus. I want to see myself, in my institute, in the church, all within the framework of the life and death and resurrection of Jesus. How can I do that? I need some kind of process categories, some system or story-frame within which to situate the stories of the religious life, my institute, myself. The story-frame I need is the story of Jesus. But how do I use that story, how do I apply it to the present situation?

Life, death, resurrection. One way is to use Pierre Teilhard de Chardin's analysis of structural process. Teilhard suggests his theory of process as a hypothesis to be applied to various processes in order to understand them better. It is not a deterministic law, but a hypothetical framework. He sees the life of the Christian, for example, in terms of three phases or dialectical movements. The first movement is *integration*. With the Lord's help, I try to build my life, I grow in union with him and also as a person; I develop my talents according to my circumstances; I integrate my life, make something out of myself, build a wholeness and an integral reality that is my life. And then I die. This is the second dialectical movement: *coming apart*, dying, being destroyed, separating into fragments, fragmentation. The third movement is *re-integration*. After my death, the Lord puts me together again, different and better, totally centered on him. He uses the fragmentation that is my death to rearrange the parts of myself into a higher synthesis, more centered on him. Integration, coming apart, re-integration. This is, of course, the dialectic of the life, death and resurrection of Jesus. My life is a sharing in his. My death participates in his death, finds its meaning in his death which has made of death a passage to new life. And my life in glory will be in the structure of his glorious risen existence.

My daily life has its crosses, too. I try to work, pray, build up my life in the Lord, integrate things, get my life together. The cross intervenes – sickness, old age, misunderstanding, failure, set-backs at the moral and psychological and physical and community levels. The cross breaks me up into pieces, partly destroys what I have built up. The Lord uses my brokenness to put me together again, this time in a higher synthesis, centered less on myself and more on him. So, by carrying my cross, I grow in union with the Lord – through darkness in prayer, through illness, through difficult interpersonal relationships, through humiliations and failures and falls. Integration, coming apart, re-integration. The world itself has the same dialectical movements. Integration: the entire history of the world, building toward an end point. Coming apart: the cataclysmic end of the world, the world's death. Re-integration: The New Jerusalem, the world-to-come.

Even within history itself, we build, come apart, put things together again. Suffering is the price of progress. Changes, peaceful or violent, can bring about a new order in society. The martyr's death gives new life. Upheaval can permit a reconstruction of society on a potentially better basis.

Life, death, resurrection of a religious institute. So too, every religious order and congregation follows a path of dialectical movement. In a first phase, the religious institute is founded, expands, levels off, and them comes apart. For example, Ignatius Loyola founded the Jesuits. The early generations were powerful in the Spirit, accomplished great things, converted thousands, worked miracles, produced outstanding contemplatives. Then, gradually, the letter replaced the Spirit, the Society of Jesus entered into the normative phase, levelled off, institutionalized its original charisms. Then it was suppressed, came apart prematurely. It began again, refounded by Joseph Pignatelli, prospered, levelled off in a new institutionalization, and became the Jesuit order that entered in 1950. In the 1960s, the order began to come apart. The present crisis consists precisely of that: we Jesuits are in the "coming apart" phase. All the difficulties, the fall in vocations, the defections, the problems with the Vatican, the restlessness – all these indicate that we are in crisis, suffering, on the cross with Jesus. Where are we going? What meaning has all this suffering?

In the structure of the cross of Jesus, the Jesuit order is dying, undergoing the normal death that comes to an end of a long life. Do not be misled by all the good that has happened in the last twenty years. The Jesuits have made a remarkable return to their original charism, not only in promulgated spirituality, but in life, in style of living, in apostolate, even in prayer. Furthermore, we have just as remarkably adapted to the present age; witness the emphasis on social justice, on peace and on dialogue with the world, with those we serve, among ourselves. Paradoxically, this great progress not only coincides with the society's "coming apart," with its present critical state, but it goes right with it. The fragmentation of the order has permitted renewal in the form of return to the original charism and in the form of adaptation to contemporary conditions. In the midst of a real, authentic, positive renewal of the order, we are dying.

The structures have been renewed, but the order is dying. This is true of so many religious orders and congregations. Some blame those who resist renewal. Whose fault is it? As far as I can see, no one's. It is simply a fact of life: whatever is born and grows, finally dies. And our orders and congregations are dying, even in the midst of the renewal of their structures – of their spirituality, of their life-style, of their apostolates, of their government.

Not all congregations are dying. Mother Teresa of Calcutta's Missionaries of Charity are still in their first generation, the generation of full-blown charisms, of great works, of growth and expansion. A number of smaller congregations and new monasteries find themselves in the same situation. They are newborn, and eventually they will level off, become more institutionalized, and finally come apart. But most of us belong to old orders and congregations. Can we save ourselves? Do we have to die? No. We do not have to die. But *we* cannot save ourselves. Only the Lord can save us.

The re-birth of the religious life. The second dialectical movement can well be followed by the third: *integration* (where we have been), *coming apart* (where we are now), *re-integration* (where we hope to be going). What shape will the re-integration of the religious life take? What will the re-integration of a particular religious institute look like? And how will it come about, if it does? The form that the third dialectical movement will take for those institutes now in the second – in crisis, fragmenting – is that of re-birth, of re-foundation, of a new beginning. Institutes now dying – not all of them, but some – will be re-founded and will begin the cycle anew: re-foundation, growth and expansion, levelling off and

institutionalization of the charisms of the re-
foundation period, and then finally: coming apart and
dying, perhaps to be re-founded again.

How will this happen? Not by meetings, whether
high level meetings or middle or low level meetings,
not by the distribution of mimeographed descriptions of
our charism, and not by questionnaires. And neither
will it happen by chapters or general congregations or
directives or legislation. All these can be good, can
help us. But re-foundation does not depend on them.

> *'Not by might, nor by power, but by my
> Spirit ' says the Lord.*
>
> Zec 4:6

Re-foundation depends on the Lord's Spirit. It
depends on whether or not a sufficient number of
persons of a given institute open their hearts to the
Lord and to his Holy Spirit and become renewed in the
Spirit, in the charisms of poverty and chastity and
obedience, in the charism of the institute, and in that
particular charism that is their own personal
vocation. Those people will find one another. They
will pray with and over one another. They can be – in
God's providence and according to his plan – the
beginning of the re-foundation of their religious
institute and the beginning of the resurrection of the
religious life.

> *Behold, they say, 'Our bones are dried up,
> and our hope is lost; we are clean cut off.'
> Therefore prophesy, and say to them,
> 'Thus says the Lord God: Behold: I will
> open your graves, and raise you from
> your graves... and I will put my Spirit
> within you, and you shall live.'*
>
> Ez 37:11-14

Lord Jesus, I put myself entirely in your hands.
Help me to see and to understand what is happening
in the religious life, in my own institute, in myself.

Show me what you are doing in my life and in my community. And help me to cooperate with you in your work in me and in my community.

Help me to understand, in terms of your own suffering and death, the sufferings and deaths in my life and the suffering and the death in my community. Teach me your ways. Make me a building-block of your new temple of the religious life of the future. Let me be a member – or at least a precursor – of the first generation of my to-be-newly-founded institute. Choose me to build on.

I am afraid to suffer, but I trust in you for the courage I need. I am afraid to speak and to act, but I trust in the guidance of your Spirit to lead me to speak and to act when you want me to.

Pour out your Holy Spirit on me so that I become a channel of your Spirit for my community.

Chapter 9

The Revolution of the Cross

The previous chapter outlines the change process in the religious life using the dialectical categories of Pierre Teilhard de Chardin. This chapter tries to do the same thing, understand better the recent and current change in the religious life, using the dialectical categories of the central section of Paul's letter to the Romans.

In order to understand better the crisis and the suffering in any order or congregation I can try to understand my institute as in the structure of the cross of Jesus. I can begin with the fact of the suffering in my religious order, the suffering not only of persons but of whole provinces, and of the whole institute and I can try to understand the suffering and the crisis in terms of the cross.

The letter to the Romans describes the event of the cross in theological categories that can help me. It talks about the cross of Christ, and about our share in the cross, in terms of story, of development. And so it can help me to make sense of the present crisis in the story of my institute.

The heart of the letter to the Romans, chapters 5–8, contains a twofold movement. The first part of this twofold movement involves a master-slave relationship, in which the master is sin and we are the slaves. The second part consists of a dynamic relationship of complementarity between God and us, a relationship that exists in the saving action of Jesus Christ, and that takes place in our lives according to

our relationship with Jesus Christ through the Holy
Spirit.

A relationship can be either positive, based on love,
or negative, based on exploitation. A negative
relationship can be called a "master-slave"
relationship; it is a union in which the dominant
member uses the other member as an object,
exploiting the other and appropriating the fruit of the
labor of the other (the exploited). Human relationships
in any society are never all positive, never all
complementary; there are always master-slave
relationships in which persons use other persons not
as subjects but as objects to be manipulated for the
benefit of the user. This is the fact of sin.

Romans 5:12 describes the master-slave relationship between sin and us. Before Jesus Christ, human
existence is in the objective structure of sin; we are
slaves in sin. As a result, we all sin; our "works" or
"work" is sin. And the product of our work, the wages
of sin, is death. Verse 13, anticipating verse 20 and
chapter 7, speaks of the Law; the Law is the rational
objectification of our situation of alienation. Under
sin, as slaves of sin, we are alienated from God, from
the world, and from ourselves. The Law puts this
alienation in words and, in a certain sense, makes it
worse. Before the Law, we are not so aware of our
sinful situation. But the Law rationally describes that
situation of sin and so makes us aware of our condition
and of our sins. We are more guilty than before,
because now we know what we do; the Law has made
our sins clear, but it has not saved us from sin.

Verses 14–20 continue to speak of the relationship
between sin and us, but only to bring about, by
contrast, the relationship of complementarity between
God and us in Jesus Christ. God unites himself with
us and our world in the incarnation, in the person of
Jesus. The work that God does in and through Jesus
is "the obedience of the one man" (verse 19). It is:
"what was done by the one man, Jesus Christ" (verse
17). This work is Jesus' death on the cross.

The work that God does, in union with us in and
through Jesus, is the work of a dynamic positive

relationship. But the work that God does, in his complementary positive relationship with us in and through Jesus, takes place in the context of the master-slave relationship in which we find ourselves, in a situation of alienation from God in which the only wages of our work (sin) is death. These two processes, the process of God uniting us to himself in Jesus in a complementary (positive) relationship, and the process of sinning in a master-slave (negative) relationship, meet at the point of "work." God's work (our salvation in Jesus) and our work (sin) meet in Jesus' work – his death on the cross.

Jesus' work of the cross is a revolution. It reverses the structures. It ends the reign of sin through death, and it creates a whole new order of grace.

> *Just as sin ruled by means of death, so also God's grace rules through righteousness.*
>
> Rom 5:21

The revolution of the cross is not so much what Jesus underwent, what he suffered, as it is what he did, a positive act, a real revolutionary work. Chapters 6, 7 and 8 of Romans describe our participation in the revolution of the cross in the new order of grace.

Chapter 6 describes Christian life as in the structure of the death of Jesus on the cross.

> *When we were baptized into union with Jesus Christ, we were baptized into union with his death.*
>
> Rom 6:3

> *Our old existence has been put to death with Christ on his cross,...so that we should no longer be slaves of sin.*
>
> Rom 6:6

Living in the structure of the cross, we are called to take responsibility, to participate in the work of the cross and to be dead to the works of sin.

*At one time you were slaves to sin. You
were set free from sin to become the
servants of righteousness.*

Rom 6:17-18

Our new life in Jesus leads to eternal life, to the
ultimate new order of the resurrection.

Chapter 7 describes the role of the Law in the
master-slave relationship. The Law objectifies for me
what I should be but am not. So I realize through the
Law that I am alienated from what I should be. I
understand that I am a sinner.

*If it had not been for the Law, I should not
have known sin.*

Rom 7:7

Knowledge of the Law only increases my
responsibility and so my guilt. Further, too weak to
fully observe the Law, I rebel, rejecting the Law. The
Law multiplies sin.

The resolution of this conflict is the content of
Chapter 8.

*For God has done what the Law,
weakened by the flesh, could not do.*

Rom 8:3

He sent Jesus to defeat and do away with sin. To do
this, he has sent us his Holy Spirit. In a union of
complementarity with the Spirit, we participate in the
sin – and death – defeating revolution of the cross.
The Spirit works in us, empowers us, frees us and
prays in us and produces fruit in our union with him.

Religious life today. The real revolution is the
cross. In my religious institute today we are in that
revolution, on the cross that leads to resurrection. I
am part of a "master-slave" relationship. I am, to
some extent, a slave of sin, of my own sinful
tendencies; I am a slave of my pride and my
sensuality, and also of my fears and my dis-

couragement and my feelings of guilt. I have my institute's spirituality, its particular interpretation of gospel discipleship, formulated in our constitutions and in the various rules and decrees we try to live by. This will not save me. It tells me *what* I should do and, above all, be. But it cannot empower me to do and to be what I am called to. For a while, the Law supported me. I had the community structures to hold me up and to keep me in place. But they never empowered me. They merely kept me in line.

Through my relationship of complementarity with the Lord, I have grown. Through the "works" of my spiritual life – prayer, asceticism, trying to live the religious life in union with Jesus Christ who calls me to follow him – I have grown in spiritual strength. And I have grown in the understanding of my vocation. There is much more to it than "keeping the rules," than "Law." This "more-to-it" is really what I am called to do and to be: to follow Jesus according to the charisms of my institute, according to its spirit and spirituality. Growth in understanding my vocation led me to turn more and more to the Lord in a kind of helplessness.

Finally, the revolution took place. At some point, the Lord entered my life in a new and special way, through a new and transforming outpouring of his Holy Spirit. My life was revolutionized by the power of the Spirit of Jesus. And this does not apply only to me, or only to members of my particular institute. It is what the Lord is doing to many religious.

Up until shortly after the Second Vatican Council, religious, especially in the more developed countries, lived for the most part "under the Law" according to rules, regulations, strict daily order, uniformity of dress – all the props of the Law. The rules taught us, formed us, held us together but they did not empower us to live up to those very rules, to that same Law. The structural renewal of the religious life has made matters both worse and better. Worse because it took away many of the props that held us up; now we do not have even the Law, except in a residual form. The absence of Law has led some to seek the Law in new forms: psychology, or sociology, or liberation theology, for example. Better because structural renewal has weakened the hold of the Law on us and made our freedom from Law a real possibility. Better also because the removal of the support of Law has led us to turn more to the Lord in personal prayer.

My institute is more consciously entering into the structure of the cross of Jesus. It is suffering, in crisis, even dying in some places. A death that is truly in the structure of the cross of Jesus can be a revolution, a salvation, a death that leads to a kind of resurrection, a new beginning. It depends on our interior life. It depends finally, on the outpouring of the empowering Spirit of Jesus.

> Come, Holy Spirit.
> Come, Lord Jesus.
>   Amen

Chapter 10

What Can I Do?

Many of our religious institutes seem to be coming to the end of a cycle, to be finishing a phase, to fall apart, to prepare to die. What can I do?

Sisters and brothers, let us not think of ourselves as the last participants in the phase coming to an end, but as the first generation of a newly beginning reality: the refoundation of our institutes.

In the Old Testament, God reveals himself as rebuilder. He wants now to rebuild the temple of my institute. How can I build with the Lord?

(1)   I can pray regularly with one or a few brothers or sisters, using the gifts the Lord has given me, and sharing what the Lord has done in my life, and how I have responded, since the last meeting. We can pray with one another for whatever graces and healings we need, meet regularly for a fixed time, say every week for an hour.

(2)   I can pray regularly with one or a few brothers or sisters, not just *for*, but *over*, following the traditional Roman Catholic custom of laying on of hands.

(3)   I can propose to my local community, if it seems prudent and feasible, that we meet regularly to share what the Lord has done

for each of us and to praise him for that together.

Lord Jesus, guide me and lead me. Show me what you want me to do so that I can live more completely for you.

Pour out on me, in a new way and in greater abundance, the graces and the charisms of the religious life according to the spirit of my institute.

Show me how you want me to share my life and to pray for the graces I need, and show me who you want me to pray with.

Make me a living stone in the rebuilding of the temple of my religious institute.

Thank you, Lord Jesus.

Amen.

Acknowledgements
and
Notes

We want to thank Sister Lucy Rooney, SND de N, for her help in going over the manuscript of this book, correcting it, and getting it in order. We thank too, Leslie Wearne for going through and correcting the first draft and typing the manuscript.

Father Faricy wrote most of Chapters 1, 7, 8 and 9. Sister Scholastica wrote most of Chapters 2, 4 and 6. We wrote Chapters 3, 5 and 10 together. There is some of each of us in every chapter.

The book is based on our personal experiences in our own religious communities, and also on our experiences with religious men and women in several countries, especially in Italy, Great Britain and the United States.

ANOTHER BEST SELLER
FROM
RESURRECTION PRESS

===

His Healing Touch

by

Msgr. Michael Buckley

This powerful book brings alive the message of healing that
Christ first gave us in the Gospels, and shows how it can
affect our lives. The author describes how the powers of love
heal not only the body but the suffering of mind and spirit,
and our broken relationships with others and with our God.

*"One of the most balanced and practical books on healing
that I have come across. His insights into healing and its
power and place within the Christian's lifestyle struck me
as right on target."* Fr. Chris Aridas

ISBN 187-871-8045   192 pp. $7.95

Order from: Resurrection Press, Ltd.
                          P.O. Box 248
                   Williston Park, NY 11596
                        (516) 742-5686

===

ANOTHER BEST SELLER
FROM
RESURRECTION PRESS

From the Weaver's Loom
Reflections on the Sundays and Feasts

by

Donald Hanson

Each reflection in this sensitive book weaves, together threads of various textures and hues: an understanding of the scripture passages; the rhythm and tone of each Sunday and feast; the cores of our struggles, hopes and dreams. A thought-provoking source for meditation and invaluable inspiration for homilies; the author transforms a vital pastoral function into a beautiful work of art.

"Sets forth the mysteries of faith in a compelling and artistic fashion." Fr. Ronald Krisman

"A book you'll want to keep handy." Fr. Ronald Hayde

ISBN 187-871-8010   160 pp. $7.95

Order from: Resurrection Press, Ltd.
P.O. Box 248
Williston Park, NY 11596
(516) 742-5686

ANOTHER BEST SELLER
FROM
RESURRECTION PRESS

A Path to Hope
for Parents of Aborted Children
and Those Who Minister to Them

by

John J. Dillon

Drawing on his considerable experience with parents of aborted children, Fr. Dillon describes the spiritual and psychological aftermath of abortion and offers solid guidelines and compassionate advice to those who counsel, minister to or journey with them.

"One of the most valuable resources available on the complexities of abortion." Fr. Gerald Twomey

"Fr. Dillon proves himself a gifted and experienced counselor in this field." THE PRIEST

ISBN 187-871-8002   80 pp. $5.95

Order from: Resurrection Press, Ltd.
P.O. Box 248
Williston Park, NY 11596
(516) 742-5686

ALSO AVAILABLE FROM
RESURRECTION PRESS

Our **Spirit Life Collection** of audiocassettes brings you the most up-to-date information on religious, ethical and moral issues. Listening at home or in the car – alone or in a group – will uplift, educate and challenge you to walk the walk of committed discipleship.

Celebrating the Vision of Vatican II

Rev. Michael J. Himes, Ph.D.

In this stimulating and humorous presentation, Michael Himes draws from the great poets and theologians of the past to weave a historical review of the Church. Looking to the future, he challenges us to continue the spirit of Vatican II "where everybody is invited to participate in the talk, in mutual love, motivated by hope and faith."

"An exceptionally perceptive and hopeful presentation of the future of Catholicism." Anthony Padovano

Michael Himes, a nationally known scholar, author and speaker, is currently an Associate Professor of Theology at Notre Dame University.

SLC90-105   60 min. $6.95

ALSO AVAILABLE FROM
OUR SPIRIT LIFE COLLECTION

Praying On Your Feet

A Contemporary Spirituality for Active Christians

Fr. Robert Lauder

Ever felt guilty about being too busy to pray? Here is the personal witness of a busy priest who struggled with this question until he realized that all Christian action is prayer and all prayer is a form of Christian action. Fr. Lauder assures us that spirituality in today's world can be achieved on our feet as well as on our knees.

SLC89-101   45 min. $6.95

Hail Virgin Mother!

A Tribute to Mary

Robert E. Lauder

In his second tape for the Spirit-Life Collection, Father Robert Lauder focuses on Mary as the first believer and disciple and as the prime communicator of faith and faithfulness. He paints a true and full picture of the Virgin Mother for our greater appreciation of the mystery and meaning of the motherhood of God.

SLC90-104   60 min. $6.95

We hope you enjoyed this book.

To receive our full brochure and to be added to
our mailing list please write:

Resurrection Press, Ltd.
P.O. Box 248
Williston Park, NY 11596